Philip Kerr's 30 Trends in ELT

Cambridge Handbooks for Language Teachers

This series, now with over 50 titles, offers practical ideas, techniques and activities for the teaching of English and other languages, providing inspiration for both teachers and trainers.

The Pocket Editions come in a handy, pocket-sized format and are crammed full of tips and ideas from experienced English language teaching professionals, to enrich your teaching practice.

Recent titles in this series:

Philip Kerr's
30 Trends
in ELT

Philip Kerr

Consultant and editor: Scott Thornbury

CAMBRIDGE
UNIVERSITY PRESS & ASSESSMENT

Shaftesbury Road, Cambridge CB2 8EA, United Kingdom

One Liberty Plaza, 20th Floor, New York, NY 10006, USA

477 Williamstown Road, Port Melbourne, VIC 3207, Australia

314–321, 3rd Floor, Plot 3, Splendor Forum, Jasola District Centre, New Delhi – 110025, India

103 Penang Road, #05–06/07, Visioncrest Commercial, Singapore 238467

Cambridge University Press & Assessment is a department of the University of Cambridge.

We share the University's mission to contribute to society through the pursuit of education, learning and research at the highest international levels of excellence.

www.cambridge.org
Information on this title: www.cambridge.org/9781009073721

First published 2022

20 19 18 17 16 15 14 13 12 11 10 9 8 7 6 5 4 3 2

Printed in Great Britain by CPI Group (UK) Ltd, Croydon CR0 4YY

A catalogue record for this publication is available from the British Library

ISBN 978-1-009-07372-1 Paperback
ISBN 978-1-009-07375-2 eBooks.com ebook

Additional resources for this publication at www.cambridge.org/delange

Contents

Acknowledgements

The authors and publishers acknowledge the following sources of copyright material and are grateful for the permissions granted. While every effort has been made, it has not always been possible to identify the sources of all the material used, or to trace all copyright holders. If any omissions are brought to our notice, we will be happy to include the appropriate acknowledgements on reprinting and in the next update to the digital edition, as applicable.

Key: U = Unit.

Text
U20: Text taken from "CEFR Companion Volume with New Descriptors Common European Framework Of Reference For Languages: Learning, Teaching, Assessment". Copyright © 2018 Council of Europe. Reproduced with kind permission of Council of Europe.

Typeset
Typesetting by QBS Learning.

Thanks

For asking interesting questions over so many years, for decades of inspiring writing, and for suggesting (and then editing) this volume, my greatest thanks go to Scott Thornbury. Sincere thanks also go to Karen Momber and Jo Timerick at Cambridge for their contributions and support, and to Alison Sharpe for her editing.

Thanks, too, to AE for being such a valuable sounding board. Finally, I'd like to express my gratitude to colleagues at The Bridge in Bratislava for sharing their views on many of the topics of this book.

Why I wrote this book

Language teaching trends and teacher development

The desire of teachers to keep up to date with new developments in English language learning and teaching is reflected in the number of conferences, teacher development events and articles with titles like *Current Trends in ELT*, *Innovate ELT*, or, to use a currently fashionable word, *Reimagining ELT Practices*. Innovation is celebrated in the titles of coursebooks like *Cutting Edge* and *Innovations*, and rewarded in the annual British Council ELTons Innovation Awards. Both inside and outside the world of ELT, it seems that everyone wants to be associated with 'innovation' (Winner, 2018).

Besides the possibility that innovations may offer something of lasting value, the promise of the 'new' is a driving force in teacher development: it '… enhances teachers' careers and prevents "burn-out"' (Hamilton, 1996). When I began teaching, in the 1980s, it was the latest trends that enthused and energised me. These included the use of corpora to study language and the development of new dictionaries like Cobuild, ongoing debates about communicative teaching and the emergence of task-based language learning, the inclusion of skills development in learning materials, self-access centres and reflective practice.

I have no doubt that my interest in areas such as these had a profound influence on my teaching, although none of them quite provided the answers to the questions I was asking. But perhaps teacher development is more about asking questions than finding answers, more about being sceptical than accepting ready-made solutions. I hope that the trends that I consider in this book will help you to formulate valuable questions about your own work, to encourage you to try something new and to continue along your own path of development.

Old current trends

However natural and important this interest in educational current trends may now seem to us, it may come as a surprise to learn that current trends have not always attracted the same attention as they do now. In the US, things really took off during the Cold War in the 1960s, when the country was spooked by Soviet technological success with Sputnik and launching Yuri Gagarin into space. Education took on a new importance as a way of boosting the skills of the workforce, of building the economy and of strengthening national security. The greatest interest was in technological advances in education – television and computers – and huge research resources were poured into these areas.

A concern with innovations in language learning and teaching lagged behind innovations in scientific and technological education, but accelerated in the late 1980s. The focus of interest, however, found its inspiration in new insights coming from the rapidly developing field of applied linguistics. Articles by authors like Diane Larsen-Freeman (1987) and Louis Alexander (1990), the most successful coursebook author of the day, were concerned with curricular questions (e.g. the relative importance of grammar and vocabulary) and new methodologies (e.g. the Communicative Approach, the Silent Way and Suggestopedia). Technology, in the form of language laboratories, was only a side-show. Thirty years later, these areas continue to feature in ELT development courses.

Since that time, interest in current trends in ELT has grown and grown. For this book, I have identified thirty trends by looking at ELT discourse from recent years that is intended for *teachers* (as opposed to researchers): ELT conference programmes, magazines for teachers (e.g. *EFL Magazine*, *English Teaching Forum*), newsletters for teachers (e.g. *IATEFL Voices*, *TESOL Connections*) and blogs (especially publishers' blogs).

The selection of trends for inclusion is, inevitably, a subjective choice. Differentiating a current trend from a dated or a largely abandoned one depends on specific ELT contexts. I have omitted a number of areas that might still be considered 'current' in some contexts because (1) they have been widely discussed and critiqued elsewhere, and (2) I feel that I have nothing of interest to add. These include things like task-based learning (TBL), the Lexical Approach, Dogme, the use of corpora, learning styles and Multiple Intelligences Theory.

Comparing old and new

A lot can still be learnt from close attention to past areas of interest, even those that might now be described as 'fringe methodologies'

(Alexander, 1990). Significant traces remain in everyday current practices. A more detailed discussion can be found in *Scott Thornbury's 30 Language Teaching Methods* (Thornbury, 2017). It is also instructive to make comparisons between the set of trends that are outlined in this book and those of the past, because this can reveal much about the (usually) unspoken assumptions and values that underpin contemporary approaches to language teaching.

The first of these, as mentioned above, concerns trends themselves. *Trends* and *innovations* are often used interchangeably, but the connotations are rather different. Since about 1945, the word *innovations* has most commonly been used to refer to technology and the value of technology in promoting economic growth. It became especially popular from the 1960s onwards. *Trends* was always a more general term. At the start of the 21st century, *innovations* overtook *trends* in terms of its frequency of use, reflecting the fact that new trends were mostly technological in nature. As we will see, current trends in ELT are now overwhelmingly oriented to technological developments.

Secondly, innovations are now commonly taken to be better than what came before, simply because they are new. In language teaching, this is rather different from the situation thirty or more years ago. Then, new ways of talking about language and teaching were more often offered as potential avenues of exploration (the term 'exploratory practice', associated with the work of Allwright (2003), started to become widely used at the end of the 20th century). Now, in contrast, trends/innovations tend to be reported much more enthusiastically, presented as things to be implemented, as opposed to explored. This is despite the fact that many, if not most, of the trends described here lack precise or generally agreed definitions.

It is also noteworthy that the ELT trends of the day thirty years ago were mostly inspired by developments in applied linguistics. This is far less the case today where inspiration is more often drawn from ideas in general education. They are explored in the teaching of other subjects before they are exported into language teaching.

Uptake of new trends also now takes place more rapidly and on a more global scale than was the case in the past. Adrian Holliday (1994) argued that approaches to language teaching that evolved in language schools and universities in Britain, Australasia and North America were promoted in state-sponsored education in countries around the world. It would appear that this trend has now been reversed to some extent.

Adoption of new ideas takes place, in part, because of their intrinsic appeal: they seem to make good sense. But adoption is also accelerated with strong financial backing. The initial funding of many contemporary educational innovations came from Silicon Valley investments, including those of the Bill and Melinda Gates Foundation and the Chan Zuckerberg Initiative. This is true not only of technological developments, such as platforms, learning analytics and adaptive learning. It is also the case for areas like 21st century skills and social-emotional learning (such as wellbeing and mindfulness). International organisations, like the OECD and the World Bank, whose primary concern is the development of human capital and who devote large portions of their budgets to education, were not slow to promote these ideas enthusiastically. With very few exceptions, national governments now also subscribe, and national education plans reflect these trends.

My interest in current trends in ELT, then, goes beyond the individual trends themselves. It is also an attempt to sketch the world of language teaching more broadly, an attempt to understand better so many of the things that we take for granted.

How to read this book

The thirty trends that I outline have been divided into three main categories: language, learning and teaching. There is a great deal of overlap between these categories, especially between learning and teaching. There is also considerable overlap between the topics of individual chapters. Whilst you could read this book in sequence, there is no need to do so. Feel free to start anywhere and roam around. In many chapters, you will find links to others, so you may wish to follow those as a route.

In discussing each trend, I provide suggestions for further reading. These include sources of practical ideas, as well as a small number of references to research evidence. The growing interest in research-based evidence is also a relatively new direction for language teaching, but, in some ways, it is no less problematic than any of the other trends. The last chapter of the book is devoted to 'evidence', but you may find that it's as good a place to start as it is to end!

Alexander, L. (1990). Fads and fashions in English language teaching. *English Today*, 6(1): pp. 35–56.

Allwright, D. (2003). Exploratory Practice: rethinking practitioner research in language teaching. *Language Teaching Research*, 7(2): pp. 113–141.

Hamilton, J. (1996). *Inspiring Innovations in Language Teaching*. Clevedon: Multilingual Matters.

Holliday, A. (1994). *Appropriate Methodology and Social Context*. Cambridge: Cambridge University Press.

Larsen-Freeman, D. (1987). Recent Innovations in Language Teaching Methodology. *The Annals of the American Academy of Political and Social Science. Vol. 90, Foreign Language Instruction: A National Agenda*, pp. 51–69.

Thornbury, S. (2017). *Scott Thornbury's 30 Language Teaching Methods*. Cambridge: Cambridge University Press.

Winner, L. (2018). The Cult of Innovation: Its Myths and Rituals. In: Subrahmanian E., Odumosu, T. and Tsao, J. (Eds.) *Engineering a Better Future*: pp. 61–73. Springer, Cham. https://doi.org/10.1007/978-3-319-91134-2_8

A: Rethinking language

This first section looks at new ways of thinking about language in educational settings. This includes the kinds of language skills and the kinds of English that are important for contemporary learners, the relationship between English and other languages, and the integration of English into the curriculum.

Plurilingualism

> Plurilingualism, sometimes referred to as multilingualism,
> holds out the promise of a more inclusive (see 6) approach
> to language learning, and challenges many accepted
> attitudes and practices.

What and why?

We live in an increasingly multilingual and multicultural world.
About 40 percent of the people in my own home city, for example,
have what is called *a migration background*. Serbian and Turkish are
commonly heard, as is English in areas with business, diplomatic,
tourist, cultural or refugee centres. Strictly monolingual speakers of
German, the language of the state, are in a minority. To communicate
in this multilingual and multicultural city, people often need to draw on
a range of plurilingual skills: they switch from one language to another
and they help others who do not have the same plurilingual skills.

Recognising the linguistic and cultural reality of much of Europe, many
European countries have officially adopted a plurilingual approach to
education (Council of Europe, 2018) in the belief that such an approach
can promote participation in democratic and social processes. It is also
hoped that it can mitigate negative responses to encounters with the
unknown (e.g. racism) and encourage participation in other cultures.
Countries elsewhere have followed suit.

In a plurilingual approach to English language learning, an imagined
'native speaker' standard of English is no longer seen as the goal to be
striven towards. Instead, the goal is a broader range of linguistic and
intercultural skills which all require some knowledge of English. The
focus has moved towards a concern with what we *do* with language in
our real-life multicultural worlds. These social functions often involve at
least two languages.

The learner may be learning English as a third, fourth or fifth language
and all these linguistic resources are seen to be of rich potential for

further learning. The taboo on using L1 in the English classroom is broken, and a range of normal behaviours (which were previously frowned upon) can be added to classroom practice. These include:

- switching between English and other languages
- spoken or written translation
- translanguaging – the use of *all* one's linguistic resources to communicate.

Translanguaging is a feature of most English classrooms. Institutions try to ban it, but have mixed success in class, and none outside. When handled sensitively and proactively, however, it may help learners' autonomy, engagement and self-esteem. It can also be a very inclusive practice (see **6**).

Learning activities which involve mediation (see **3**) between two or more languages (e.g. a text in one language and a summary in another) are considered an important part of the learning diet.

Taking a plurilingual approach further, imagine a classroom in Australia: it's full of newly-arrived students from all over the world. For some of them, schooling was severely disrupted and the possibility of future advanced study may seem very remote. Together these EAL learners explore, through texts, aspects of each other's backgrounds and of Australia, using all their plurilingual resources to do so.

In practice

It's one thing to sign up to an international policy initiative. It's quite another to enact it with enthusiasm. In national language policies and the organisation of school curricula, in formal assessment criteria of language skills, and the privileges given to 'native speakers', we see little that is really plurilingual in orientation. More commonly, we see the other languages and English treated as discrete entities that should not mix.

There are many ways of assessing someone's English language skills, but in schools, universities and high-stake exams, evaluating plurilingual skills (along with English) is relatively rare. More often, students are evaluated with reference to a set of monolingual norms, and they are not best advised to start switching from one language to another during their exams.

There are, however, contexts where plurilingual practices are more likely to be the norm. In some forms of both bilingual education and Content and Language Integrated Learning (CLIL) (see 4), plurilingualism may be very visible. But in general English classes (in high school, for example), plurilingualism is up against the exam system. Ways of measuring plurilingual skills exist, but there is strong resistance to the idea and they are not easily standardised internationally. Compartmentalising English as entirely separate from other languages is what most people are used to. Attitudes die hard.

Attitudes have, however, softened in recent years in some places. There is a growing acceptance of the important role of the L1 in learning English, although this is far from universal. Translation exercises are no longer the preserve of a few old-fashioned teachers. They have become a core feature of many online language learning tools. The findings of English as a Lingua Franca researchers (see 2) are also beginning to be reflected in the design of materials with language models of more diverse kinds. This is particularly the case with listening and pronunciation materials, less so with models of written language. Finally, the official importance accorded to interlingual mediation (see 3) means that it is increasingly hard to keep the English language classroom free of the 'other' language(s).

Takeaways

Since I have written a book of practical ideas for incorporating own-language activities in the English classroom (Kerr, 2014), it'll come as no surprise to find out that I don't think that English is always best learnt in an English-only environment. But using the L1 (and other languages) from time to time to aid the acquisition of English is not really the same thing as pursuing a plurilingual approach.

I first taught English in a Moroccan lycée, where French, Arabic and Šəlḥa were all used and heard. It would have been an ideal setting for a plurilingual approach, but the students I taught were mostly pretty good at translanguaging already – even though the term hadn't been coined yet. What they needed was a level of written standardised Arabic, French and English to get through their baccalauréat. Keeping English separate from home languages, and employing native-speaker teachers like me, were thought to be good ways of achieving the goals set by the ministry, whose thinking had not been influenced by the 'Multilingual Turn' in applied linguistics. This only came in the second decade of the 21st century, some 25 years later.

The plurilingual/multilingual practices and attitudes that have been experimented with in recent years are certainly more inclusive than what came before, and it may be that there are other advantages – increases in learner motivation, agency and metacognition (see 28), for example. But we also know that plurilingual competence develops by itself. Plurilingual instruction may help it along.

Canagarajah, S. (2013). *Translingual Practice: Global Englishes and Cosmopolitan Relations*. New York: Routledge.

Kerr, P. (2014). *Translation and Own-Language Activities*. Cambridge: Cambridge University Press.

May, S. (Ed.) (2014). *The Multilingual Turn*. New York: Routledge.

Narcy-Combes, M. F., Narcy-Combes, J. P., McAllister, J., Leclère, M. and Miras, G. (2019). *Language Learning and Teaching in a Multicultural World*. Bristol: Multilingual Matters.

2   English as a Lingua Franca (ELF)

> You have to keep your eye on the ball with ELF because definitions keep changing. In its latest embodiment, ELF is all about plurilingualism (see 1).

What and why?

Looking at the way that English is used as a lingua franca makes intuitive good sense since its users far outnumber its native-speakers. There is no reason to idealise 'native speakers' of a language. There is no good reason to get hung up about American, British or Australian norms. There are many reasons to be more inclusive (see 6) and an ELF-informed approach may be more tolerant and empowering for both learners and their teachers. The idea of ELF also supports those who campaign against discrimination against 'non-native' teachers of English, illegal in some countries, accepted as the norm in others.

But English as a Lingua Franca (ELF), is a slippery beast. It refers to three rather different things. In its first iteration, ELF.1, the main focus appeared to be on the language forms, especially aspects of pronunciation and lexico-grammar, that mattered for intercultural intelligibility. This soon morphed into ELF.2, where the focus shifted to *how* people of different language backgrounds used English to communicate in particular situations. And ELF.2 was, in turn, supplemented by ELF.3, which brings us to a perspective that identifies with plurilingualism/multilingualism (see 1). ELF has now been reconceptualised as 'English as a multilingual franca', and ELF scenarios may include situations where English is available to the speakers, and they may draw on their knowledge of English, but they don't actually choose to use it.

In the early years of this century, there was an explosive leap in the number of books, journals and articles about ELF. There was lively debate about ELF.1 and ELF.2, not least about the practical classroom, teacher training and assessment implications. However, twenty years after ELF became widely used as a term, ELF researchers lament the absence of any sizable changes in classroom practices.

A number of reasons for this lack of uptake may be speculated on. Two come immediately to my mind. First, native-speakerism (i.e. a bias towards native-speakers and their speech varieties) is embedded in so many systems that it's hard to know where to begin. Secondly, support from large numbers of teachers has been less enthusiastic than had been hoped for. Many, myself included, aspire to 'native-speaker' norms in languages that are not our own.

In practice

A lot of English language teaching and assessment is concerned with getting students to reproduce accurate language forms – grammatical, lexical and phonological. But without a norm against which we can measure this accuracy, teachers and test makers (especially makers of online, automatically marked tests) are left with something of a problem. Omitting a third person singular 's', for example, is highly unlikely to impede communication in an ELF (or any) setting, and it may not even be noticed. In many ways, it really doesn't matter. So, should teachers give feedback on it? Many teachers think yes, and many learners, perhaps especially adults, agree with them. The debate, going back at least six hundred years, is unlikely to be resolved any time soon.

It's fairly natural for teachers to have an interest in grammatical accuracy: getting through an accuracy-based test or two is something most have experienced on the way to becoming a teacher. Many are less interested in pronunciation: it's an open secret that pronunciation activities in coursebooks are often skipped. The first and most tangible product of ELF is the Lingua Franca Core, which includes a short list of sounds or sound pairings that are problematic in ELF settings when ELF users mix them up. It tells us, for example, that we should worry more about long and short vowels, and less about pronouncing *th*. It's a handy list, and it's beginning to be reflected in more recent coursebooks.

The Lingua Franca Core for pronunciation was a product of ELF.1. Attempts to produce similar 'cores' for grammar and vocabulary did not come to fruition, as attention shifted in ELF.2 to the pragmatic moves that users of ELF typically make. Here, again, ELF scholars have produced some handy documents: lists of the kinds of strategies that effective ELF users deploy when they are speaking. Fluent use of these strategies usually entails knowing a few set phrases, and when to use them, and this language can be taught/learnt quite easily. Examples of such speaking strategies include managing conversations (keeping it going, changing the topic, repairing misunderstandings, etc.) and being a supportive listener (checking information, responding positively, etc.).

Takeaways

The two tangible and practical artefacts of ELF I have just mentioned serve useful purposes in almost any English language classroom, but ELF, if understood as a multilingual practice (ELF.3), also challenges many of us to change our mindset more radically. Many habitual practices will need to be rethought. A good number of the practical activities in Kiczkowiak and Lowe's (2018) compendium are intended to develop an 'ELF mindset' in learners: a better understanding of the global role of English or the nonsense of native-speakerism, for example. Learners' attitudes may need shifting, too.

It is probably easiest to operate with an ELF model if you are in a bilingual educational system, if you are teaching English as an additional language in an English-speaking country, if you are a teacher of CLIL (see 4), or a teacher using English as a Medium of Instruction (see 5).

I'm none of these things, but I find the Lingua Franca Core a useful reference. Inclusion of conversational strategies in a syllabus makes sense to me, too. I'm happy to see (and hear) fewer white, middle-class 'native speaker' norms in learning material. I understand the rationale for a diminished focus on grammatical accuracy. But I'm afraid I still want to approximate closer to an imagined native speaker when I speak languages other than English.

Jenkins, J., Baker, W. and Dewey, M. (Eds.) (2018). *The Routledge Handbook of English as a Lingua Franca*. Abingdon, Oxon.: Routledge.

Kiczkowiak, M. and Lowe, R. J. (2018). *Teaching English as a Lingua Franca*. Stuttgart: DELTA Publishing.

MacKenzie, I. (2014). *English as a Lingua Franca*. Abingdon, Oxon.: Routledge.

Seidlhofer, B. (2011). *Understanding English as a Lingua Franca*. Oxford: Oxford University Press.

Interlingual mediation

3

> A big part of a language teacher's job is to mediate texts of all kinds to their learners. Much of this mediation is cross-linguistic (e.g. explaining vocabulary), and it's a skill that learners need, too.

What and why?

A common thing that we do with language is help other people understand a text of some kind which, for a variety of reasons, they may be having problems with. To do so, we may summarise or simplify it, exemplify it or provide extra details, change the register, or, in other ways make it more comprehensible. This is mediation, and the problems may be caused by the interlocutor's lack of familiarity with the type of text or the ideas and cultural references expressed in it. In a multilingual setting, the problem may arise because of language differences and, in such cases, cross-linguistic (or interlingual) mediation is needed. In addition to the mediating strategies mentioned above, this will involve elements of translation and/or use of English as a Lingua Franca (see 2). It is the focus of this chapter.

In 2018, the Council of Europe published a companion volume to their Common European Framework of Reference for Languages (see 20). Mediation featured prominently in this volume and this, more than anything else, is having an impact on language teaching and assessment practices in Europe and more globally.

The volume breaks mediation down into a series of activities and strategies. The activities include:

- relaying and summarising (either in speech or writing) information from spoken or written texts
- translating (either in speech or writing) written texts
- note-taking in lectures and meetings (which may be in another language).

The strategies include:

- linking to previous knowledge (e.g. by asking questions to activate prior knowledge)
- adapting language (e.g. by paraphrasing)
- simplifying or highlighting key information.

Mediation in the 'companion volume' is not restricted to cross-linguistic mediation, but it plays a very important role. This is a recognition of our multilingual/multicultural lives and the importance of switching between two or more languages.

In practice

The inclusion of a focus on interlingual mediation necessarily entails the abandonment of an English-only approach to teaching English. Arguments against English-only approaches are already well-established and broadly accepted by the academic community, even if still less so in some educational institutions. A summary of these can be found in my own book *Translation and Own-Language Activities* (Kerr, 2014). However, as mediation is increasingly promoted by supranational bodies and included in lists of 'global competences' (such as the Pisa 2018 Global Competence framework), it will be incorporated more and more within formal assessment practices (see, for example, the Council of Europe's website www.ecml.at/mediation). Cross-linguistic mediation tasks already feature in school-leaving examinations in a number of countries. English-only approaches will therefore become increasingly problematic.

The kinds of classroom activities that involve cross-linguistic mediation mirror the descriptions of mediation activities and strategies found in the Council of Europe (2018) 'companion volume'. It is beyond the scope of this chapter to give more than a brief glimpse of the available possibilities. A much wider selection may be found in Kerr (2014) and González Davies (2004). Here is a small selection:

- three-way bilingual roleplays, where the role cards stipulate that one bilingual speaker mediates between two other speakers who do not share a language
- presentations (in English) by individual students of interesting films, websites, etc. that are in another language

- learners read or listen to a text in English, and make notes and/or summarise in their own language
- learners expand a short English text after carrying out research in their own language
- information gap tasks where learners read (or listen to) texts in one or more other languages and share the information in English.

Mediation is also central to CLIL practices (see 4) where learners use more than one language to acquire, explore and share new knowledge and concepts. Code-switching (switching from one language to the other) and translanguaging (the process of using all one's language resources to achieve communicative goals) are likely to be standard ways of achieving mediation goals in such settings.

Takeaways

In a language classroom, the mediation of communication between teachers and learners is often a multilingual affair, sometimes reluctantly on the part of the teacher. The mediation of texts (using dictionaries, for example) and the mediation of ideas (grammar explanations, for example) are also often multilingual activities. Rather than using the other language(s) just as a fall-back option, we could embrace the potential of interlingual mediation activities more fully. These activities clearly entail an acceptance of an important role for the learners' other languages, and the implications of this need to be thought through.

The issues are both practical and curricular. If some use of other languages is accepted, or even promoted, how do we manage things to avoid excessive use? In contexts where the teachers do not share the other languages, how will they evaluate the learners' use of mediation strategies? Highlighting mediation also has the effect of underlining the importance of language as a utilitarian and transactional tool (in a multilingual world), but this brings with it the risk that more humanistic and creative uses of language are downgraded.

A certain shift in priorities is therefore unavoidable, and you or your learners may feel that it is not for you. In many contexts, however, especially those where the vocational purposes of language learning are paramount (Business English, for example), the codification of mediation skills in the CEFR companion volume can provide a very useful guide to classroom practice.

Chiappini, R. and Mansur, E. (2021). *Activities for Mediation*. Stuttgart: Delta Publishing.

Council of Europe. (2018). *Common European Framework of Reference for Languages: Learning, Teaching, Assessment: Companion Volume with New Descriptors*. Strasbourg: Council of Europe. https://rm.coe.int/cefr-companion-volume-with-new-descriptors-2018/1680787989

González Davies, M. (2004). *Multiple Voices in the Translation Classroom*. Amsterdam: John Benjamins.

Kerr, P. (2014). *Translation and Own-Language Activities*. Cambridge: Cambridge University Press.

Stathopoulou, M. (2015). *Cross-Language Mediation in Foreign Language Teaching and Testing*. Bristol: Multilingual Matters.

Content and Language Integrated Learning (CLIL)/Content-Based Instruction (CBI)

4

> Teaching learners an academic subject in an additional language (e.g. English) seems to offer rich potential. However, classroom reality is a little more complicated than a simple switch from one language to another.

What and why?

What's in a chapter heading? For some people, CLIL and CBI are very different entities. For others, there is so much overlap between them that it is not really possible to differentiate them. Still others may wonder if both CLIL and CBI should not be dealt with in the chapter on English as a Medium of Instruction (see 5), rather than getting a chapter to themselves. For myself, the big difference between CLIL and CBI is that when you walk out of a typical CLIL school classroom, you're not surrounded by the language of the classroom.

A recurrent theme of this book is that trends are, more often than not, poorly defined. CLIL is no exception. It is often referred to as an umbrella term for a variety of approaches, most of which offer a two-for-the-price-of-one deal: subject matter learning and proficiency in another language, at the same time (e.g. German-speaking high school students study engineering in English). Variations include:

- pairs of teachers working in tandem, using different languages
- one teacher switching between languages
- some classes taught in one language, some in others
- additional language classes provided for some learners.

CLIL (the more common term in Europe) approaches started spreading in Europe around the turn of the century, and, two decades later, have become the norm in many places. CLIL may have a positive impact on learner motivation, attitudes towards learning the language, and enhanced confidence. It is also generally popular with parents.

Most language teaching researchers are enthusiastic, too. In at least significant parts of CLIL lessons, students are learning a language by doing something with it, rather than learning about it, even though supplementary language-focussed study may be needed. CLIL provides a clear and authentic communicative purpose to language use, something that is often difficult to achieve in a language-focussed class. It is claimed that learners like CLIL, too, but we will need more data to verify the claim. The number of student dropouts from CLIL classes suggests the picture may be rather more complicated.

In practice

My daughter's primary school proudly displays a poster near the entrance, proclaiming, in English, 'We are a CLIL school.' In fact, half of the classes could be called CLIL, and the rest are monolingual German. The children in the CLIL classes are already bilingual (German-English, but often with another language – Hungarian, Polish or Chinese, for example) when they enter the school. The school operates a selection policy and parents of the CLIL children tend to have higher socio-economic status than parents of the non-CLIL cohort. Demographic differences like this have been observed in many CLIL contexts.

In common with most CLIL schools, English is the target language and 'CLIL' is something of a brand name. This version of CLIL has evolved as a response to both local needs and educational directives from local government, so numeracy (in German) and basic English and German *literacy* skills are the focus of the early years. In terms of classroom practices, a million miles separate it from other CLIL schools, where, for example, *spoken* skills in English are the target in engineering classes. The contexts of primary, secondary and vocational schools using CLIL vary enormously. With so many varieties of CLIL, and with no unifying approach or theory, it's very hard to say what CLIL is. And without resolving the definition, it's very hard to evaluate the effectiveness of CLIL as an approach. CLIL requires some sort of balance to be struck between the content and the language, and it is not easy to do this 50-50. Do you want your CLIL 'hard', where academic achievement is prioritised, or 'soft', where language skills are the driving force?

Putting these reservations to one side, there is some evidence that CLIL has had favourable effects on English learning. Evidence on how CLIL impacts on overall academic achievement is less readily available. The language gains may, however, be due in part simply to more hours of English. They may also be partly attributable to differences in teaching style. A tightly teacher-led class, mostly in explanatory or corrective mode, with all communication conducted through the teacher, is likely to lead to fewer language gains than a task-driven approach with learners working in groups.

Takeaways

Most commentators agree that CLIL imposes a greater workload on teachers. The workload is also greater for most learners. This means that, for both, motivation needs to be high, and this cannot be assumed. Both may need support, and institutional support may be in short supply. When children are too young to have had much say in their enrolment in a CLIL school, and when teachers have had little choice but to switch their language of instruction, attitudes may not be altogether positive.

One of the aims of the European advocates of CLIL is to promote what they see as more progressive pedagogies. It certainly aligns closely to task-based and communicative language learning. It reminds those of us not working in CLIL of the importance of having a good reason to use the language you are learning. It reminds those of us working in English-only classrooms that a healthy plurilingual alternative (see **1**) is also possible.

It may well be the case that CLIL has been somewhat oversold, but it has helped to keep alive the debates about the best ways to learn languages, and especially about the role of the L1 in that process.

Ball, P., Kelly, K. and Clegg, J. (2015). *Putting CLIL into Practice*. Oxford: Oxford University Press.

Coyle, D., Hood, P. and Marsh, D. (2010). *Content and Language Integrated Learning*. Cambridge: Cambridge University Press.

Lyster, R. (2018). *Content-Based Language Teaching*. New York: Routledge.

Mehisto, P., Marsh, D. and Frigols, M. J. (2008). *Uncovering CLIL*. London: Macmillan Education.

5

English as a Medium of Instruction (EMI)

> The teaching of academic subjects through English
> is a simple and intuitively appealing idea. Driven by
> commercial considerations, its growth has been rapid,
> but the classroom reality is complex and often much less
> successful than hoped for.

What and why?

The idea of studying school subjects in a language other than your own
has been around a long time. Think back to the days when Sumerian,
Latin or Ottoman Turkish (the languages of colonial power) were
used as a medium of instruction. These days, in universities around the
world, it is almost always English that is chosen as the international
language for teaching and study. There is a long and ugly history of
English as a medium of instruction in the context of colonial schooling,
and vestiges of this still remain.

There is no colonial connection between Britain and my home town,
but my local university offers almost thirty master programmes taught
completely in English, ranging from data science to immunobiology.
The required level is B2. This is far from unique, as the university is
competing in a global marketplace where English is the lingua franca,
and attracting international students is seen to be vital for its future. It is
a recognition that English dominates the world of academic publishing,
and the internationalisation (or rather Englishisation) of the university is
thought to enhance its prestige. EMI courses also facilitate the mobility
of both students and staff, if their English language skills are improved
through an EMI policy. The idea that EMI courses can kill two birds
with one stone, i.e. developing both academic knowledge and English
language skills, lies behind many EMI initiatives, although improvement
in English is rarely one of the stated objectives of EMI courses.

Contemporary EMI is most commonly found in universities, and this
is my focus here. It has tended to be the private universities that lead

the way. Marketing of EMI courses was helped by the English-speaking trio of the United States, Britain and Australia promoting themselves as academic superpowers. EMI continues to grow, as public universities play 'catch-up' and there is more governmental backing for them to compete in the global academic marketplace. Pressure on the secondary sector then follows, so that students are prepared for their EMI degree.

In practice

An entry level of B2 for an EMI course is not high, and the bar is often set even lower. Depending on which examination is used to determine this level, some students may also have significantly weaker productive skills in English than their examined level suggests. They may also be lacking in their competence with the local language (in my context, this is German), restricting their ability to integrate into the local community in which they find themselves.

Some universities require little, if anything, in the way of English language requirements and provide no language support for the students they enrol. Macaro (2018) refers to this as the 'ostrich model', where the institution pretends that there is no problem, or that, if there is one, it will go away of its own accord. More often, language requirements exist, although commercial pressures mean that they may not be high enough. To compensate for the lack of language skills, universities may offer either pre-sessional or in-sessional support, or a combination of the two. The former is often a year in length, and combines language development with some training in academic skills such as critical thinking (see 8). Responding to this need, international publishers have produced series of coursebooks of English for Academic Purposes (EAP), the first level of which is often targeted at A2 students. The latter, in-sessional language classes, are usually separate from the main academic curriculum, and may bring together students from a variety of disciplines, despite the fact that the language needs of students in one academic subject may be very different from those in another. It is possible to identify features of general academic English, such as word lists of high frequency academic words, but most students would benefit from an analysis of the specific language demands of their courses, and this is not always available to the tutors or it is difficult to incorporate into the general needs of an in-sessional group.

Among EMI lecturers, too, there are inevitably wide variations in their English language skills. At times, a simultaneous interpreter is needed. In some cases, lecturers have been required to upgrade their skills, but support in ways to modify their pedagogical approach to better suit EMI learners appears to be rare. These might include ways of breaking up an uninterrupted flow of lecture-mode with a range of more learner-centred tasks, training in language grading, and the use of translanguaging techniques. Unsurprisingly, many EMI lecturers feel they could do a better job in their own language. Feelings of demotivation are not uncommon, especially among those who had no choice in the switch to EMI.

Given the challenges outlined above, we should not expect research findings about the efficacy of EMI to be unequivocally positive, and the picture that emerges from EMI research is decidedly mixed. In some countries, learning of academic content has deteriorated, and drop-out rates have been high, but we do not have enough information to make global generalisations. Improvements in English language skills are also often disappointing, although a number of research reports indicate gains in listening. We cannot, however, assume that following EMI studies will lead to greater language gains than, say, attending fewer hours of an intensive English course. The idea that two birds can be killed with one stone remains speculative.

The widespread rolling-out of EMI programmes has led to concerns about a negative effect on the status of other languages. There is also a danger that EMI may exacerbate social inequalities. Those who are most likely to benefit from the approach are 'those whose life chances have already placed them in a position to benefit from education' (Macaro, 2018). It is clear that EMI has spread globally without sufficient consideration of both its benefits and its costs.

Takeaways

The rush to implement EMI is not dissimilar to enthusiasm for other trends that will be discussed in this book. Before turning to these, I would like to offer a short checklist of questions that are suggested by the lessons we can learn from EMI.

- Have we adequately anticipated potential drawbacks alongside the advantages?

- Have we evaluated the ways in which implementation of the trend might impact on questions of inclusivity and wellbeing?
- What kinds of training will be needed before the trend can realise its potential?
- Is there sufficient research evidence to justify our enthusiasm for the trend?
- Have we transferred our enthusiasm for one particular, closely defined iteration of the trend to the trend as a whole?

Galloway, N. and Rose, H. (2021). English medium instruction and the English language practitioner. *ELT Journal*, 75 (1): 33–41.

Macaro, E. (2018). *English Medium Instruction*. Oxford: Oxford University Press.

Sahan, K., Mikolajewska, A., Rose, H., Macaro, E., Searle, M., Aizawa, I., Zhou, S. and Veitch, A. (2021). *Global mapping of English as a medium of instruction in higher education: 2020 and beyond*. London: British Council.

B: Rethinking learning

We turn our attention next to ways in which English language learning is increasingly viewed as involving more than just learning the language. First, there is growing interest in the kinds of non-linguistic skills (life skills) that language learners need in the real world of work and study. Very closely related are the social-emotional skills that are known to help learning. Interest in making learning more efficient has now become inseparable from interest in educational technologies. Blended and flipped learning are included in this section because of their primary focus on *learning*. We will turn to other uses of educational technology in section C.

Language teachers bring a range of technical skills to their work, but underlying these is always a set of ethical values. Questions about inclusivity require us to reconsider these values and re-evaluate our educational priorities.

What and why?

I use the term *inclusivity* to refer to three interrelated concepts: equality, diversity, and inclusion. *Equality* here means that all learners are treated fairly and not subject to forms of discrimination, irrespective of any characteristics they may have. This entails equality of opportunity, which means that everybody has an equal chance to learn. Since some learners are more privileged than others in a variety of ways, equality of opportunity can only be realised if measures are taken to empower those lacking in privilege. *Diversity* here means that individual and group differences which affect equality are acknowledged, respected and celebrated. Characteristics which fall under this description typically include age, race, different body types, religion, cultural background, neurodiversity, disability, social class, sex, gender and sexual orientation. Many learners, of course, suffer from multiple forms of discrimination. *Inclusion*, the third of these concepts, refers to the concrete ways in which equality and diversity are realised in educational contexts.

The paragraph above reflects my own personal and cultural values, as does any discussion of equality. *Equality of opportunity* is a particularly contested term – interpreted in so many different ways – with the result that there is inevitable disagreement about what, in practical terms, inclusion should look like. In addition, particular sets of values can conflict with others. How, for example, does my belief in the importance of equality of educational opportunity sit with the belief of many socio-economically privileged parents that they have the right to select and pay for the kinds of private education that are more likely to help their children achieve high proficiency in English?

Besides the moral reasons for embracing more inclusive practices, there may also be legal reasons for doing so. Inclusive and equitable education is one of the United Nations' Sustainable Development Goals, and many countries now require school curricula to respect diversity, although the way that diversity is defined varies in significant ways.

There are also a number of reasons for embracing inclusivity that are specific to English language teaching. Among these is the close connection between learning a language and developing intercultural competence, requiring an awareness of and respect for differences both between and within cultures. Inclusive approaches therefore require attention to the selection and design of learning materials, and the teaching methodology that is deployed. Plurilingual approaches (see 1), for example, are, by design, more inclusive than strictly monolingual policies.

Reading and listening play central roles in all forms of learning, but particularly so in language learning. Inclusive language teaching needs to find ways of accommodating the needs of learners whose participation in learning activities is otherwise restricted because of differences in, for example, their sight and hearing. Similarly, a celebration of neurodiversity will likely lead to a rethinking of the appropriacy of certain activities and classroom management techniques.

In practice

The world of English language teaching is itself too diverse for us to make general observations of the ways in which inclusion is currently being enacted. There are, however, a number of recent initiatives that have received international attention, in part because of the support they have received from publishers and from the global teachers' associations, TESOL and IATEFL, both of which have special interest sections devoted to diversity and inclusivity.

It is estimated that between five and fifteen percent of people have specific learning differences, and, of these, dyslexia is one of the most common. Learning English can be challenging for everyone, but for learners with dyslexia, difficulties with reading and spelling, writing, vocabulary and grammar, may all be amplified. As a consequence, motivation and anxiety may be negatively impacted. Recent interest in supporting English language learners with dyslexia (e.g. Daloiso, 2017) is therefore important and welcome. The advice that is provided is wide-ranging, concerning everything from the design of texts and the choice of classroom activities, to fairer forms of assessment.

Digital technology has greatly facilitated the provision of learning materials appropriate to learners with differing needs (see **18**), but the spread of online learning has also brought into focus the importance of inclusion in terms of access to this technology. Without access to good affordable devices and connectivity, the potential benefits will remain elusive.

Coursebooks and other learning materials produced by international publishers have long been criticised, with justification, for being white-anglocentric, male dominated, and heteronormative, and for reflecting culturally limited, middle-class values that are often alien to the students for whom the material is intended. My own recent experience as a coursebook writer indicates that this is beginning to change, although much still remains to be done. Publishers and writers are now more sensitive to the need for greater diversity in the visual and textual representation of people and cultures. It is now quite rare to encounter newly published work that does not strive for a better mix of men and women, and of ethnicity. Models of English language are no longer provided exclusively by white native-speakers (see **2**). However, for commercial and cultural reasons, many taboos, especially LGBTQ+ related, remain.

Takeaways

The creation of materials that cater well to specific learning differences or the inclusion of visual representations of greater diversity are certainly welcome, but inclusive practices need to be more far-reaching if they are not to be tokenistic. One way of approaching inclusion in a more comprehensive way is by using a framework called Universal Design for Learning (UDL), developed by CAST. This framework notes the importance of providing multiple means of (1) engagement (the affective response to learning), (2) representation (the ways in which information is presented), and (3) action and expression (the ways in which and the media through which learners can express themselves).

Instead of focussing only on specific issues of equality, UDL allows for a more intersectional understanding of discrimination and privilege where a number of individual and social characteristics like gender, race and disability may overlap. As a lens through which we can view and respond to individual learner differences, it is of value in all language classes in all contexts.

British Council (2009). *Equal Opportunity And Diversity: The Handbook For Teachers Of English*. London: The British Council.

CAST (Center for Applied Special Technology) Website https://www.cast.org/

Daloiso, M. (2017). *Supporting Learners with Dyslexia in the ELT Classroom*. Oxford: Oxford University Press.

Smith, A. M. (Ed.) (2020). *Activities for Inclusive Language Teaching*. Stuttgart: Delta Publishing.

Lists of 21st century skills (that are needed by the youth of today) are readily available and popular with economists. Will teaching these skills help learners add value to the economy?

What and why?

Promoted massively by supranational bodies like the OECD and the World Bank, by national governments, and by technology companies, 21st century skills have become a widely accepted part of ELT curricula everywhere. Also known as life skills, global skills and soft skills, the names that are used continue to evolve, as do the precise definitions. But there is enough of a common understanding for us to avoid major confusion. These skills are thought to be those that are needed to work and live successfully in the knowledge economy of the 21st century. In practice, this is usually more about working than other aspects of life. The skills are identified by asking global businesses what kind of skills they are looking for when they hire staff. The list usually includes:

- Communication skills (e.g. making presentations, using different media to share ideas)
- Collaboration skills (e.g. working effectively with others, making compromises)
- Critical thinking and problem-solving skills (see **8**)
- Creativity and innovation skills (see **9**).

Since each of these begins with the letter 'C', people also refer to the 'Four Cs'.

People often note that there is nothing new about the importance of some of these skills. They are important in any economy. But, it is argued, they are particularly important in a digital knowledge economy, where work practices evolve fast, and where this evolution can suddenly accelerate when confronted with unpredictable events, such as a pandemic. In addition, taxonomies of 21st century skills usually include:

- Life and career skills
- Information, media, and technology skills (e.g. digital literacies, see **10**).

These skills are highly valued, and economists attempt to calculate the dollar-value that a value-added workforce can add to a national economy. It is not surprising, then, to see them assessed numerically: we need, after all, to ensure that they are taught effectively and efficiently. Frameworks (see **20**) to allow this assessment have been developed by UNICEF, the British Council, Cambridge English, and Oxford University Press, among others.

It probably makes most sense for these skills to be taught across the curriculum in an integrated way, but that is not always possible. English language classes, which are already concerned with communication skills and, to a lesser extent, collaboration skills, offer a seemingly natural home for the incorporation of content that is oriented to 21st century skills.

In practice

The idea of preparing learners for the challenges of the 21st century, or words to similar effect, proved rapidly popular with both marketing people and educators. Within a few years of the publication of the best-selling *21st Century Skills* by Trilling and Fadel (2009), ELT publishers were incorporating a 21st century skill strand to the syllabus of major coursebooks. One publisher, Macmillan, developed an online resource bank of 21st century skills material and won a British Council prize for innovation for their efforts.

At times, and especially at the start, the '21st century' content was little more than rebadged material that was already familiar. Pair work could be relabelled 'communication' and 'collaboration', and discussion tasks that were more cognitively challenging could be called 'critical thinking'.

At the same time, as part of the discussions about 21st century needs, a growing importance was also attached to 'higher-order' thinking skills (analysis, evaluation and creation), as opposed to the less cognitively challenging tasks of remembering, understanding and applying. In the classroom, this entails the prioritisation of doing 'real-life' things with language, and less of studying grammar rules. There's a wide number of possible ways of combining standard ELT activities with 21st century themes. The following examples give just a flavour:

- a text and discussion about managing distractions and time management for students
- a workplace role play followed by a discussion about the qualities of a positive team member
- a discussion about respecting other people's personal space
- a vlog project about fake news.

Takeaways

Whilst many of the activities labelled '21st century skills' have much to recommend them in terms of the opportunities they offer for meaningful language practice, the extent to which they achieve their goals of teaching particular life skills is much less clear. There are a number of reasons why it's hard to say how effective such lessons are.

A one-off lesson on, say, critical thinking or leadership skills, is unlikely to have much, if any, impact. General English courses, designed for secondary students, have a large number of skills to pick from, and, as a result, there is no systematic attempt to develop particular skills. On the whole, learners practise a variety of skills, but they don't necessarily learn how to improve them. Only when a smaller number of skills are targeted in a more organised way is there any likelihood of achieving life skills goals. Examples include critical thinking in academic English courses, or leadership skills in a business English course.

A broader concern is the degree to which some of these skills can be taught at all. It has been argued, for example, that both creativity and critical thinking are domain-specific. That is to say that an ability to be creative or to think critically in one domain or context (like mechanical engineering) doesn't necessarily transfer to a similar ability in a different domain (like football or learning psychology). Without an adequate knowledge base in any domain, you cannot really deploy any higher-order skills.

Skills are much harder to measure than knowledge about language, but without measuring gains in skills it's impossible to determine the effectiveness of activities that are designed to develop them. Before measuring, we need to define what we're measuring and here we run into the problem that everyone defines these skills slightly differently. When we dig down a little further and ask how we might define and measure individual skills, such as creative thinking (see 9), we find that this, too, can be broken down in many different ways, none of which lend themselves readily to assessment.

Finally, it is worth unpacking some of the assumptions behind the promotion of 21st century skills. The focus is on work, rather than life, and the assumption is a future world of work where, for example, entrepreneurial skills or information literacy may be relevant. Not everyone is as optimistic about the future. Some suggest that we'd be doing our students more of a favour by preparing them for a world where work is a minority occupation. Is this focus on the utilitarian or work purposes of learning English appropriate for all learners, anyway? It didn't use to be like that.

Mavridi, S. and Xerri, X. (Eds.) (2020). *English for 21st Century Skills*. Newbury, Berks.: Express Publishing.

Mercer, S., Hockly, N., Stobart, G. and Galés, N. L. (2019). *Global Skills: Creating Empowered 21st Century Citizens*. Oxford: Oxford University Press.

Trilling, B. and Fadel, C. (2009). *21st Century Skills*. San Francisco: Wiley.

> The skill of critical thinking is self-evidently a desirable
> attribute for our learners to acquire. Who could be against
> it? But to what extent can English language teachers
> promote critical thinking skills?

What and why?

Critical thinking, often in combination with problem-solving, is
regularly at or near the top of the lists of important 21st century
skills (see 7). Its empowering appeal is obvious, but nobody can
agree on precisely what it is. One review of the literature found that
critical thinking entailed the analysis of arguments, inferencing skills,
evaluation, decision-making, and problem-solving. In addition to skills
such as these, critical thinking requires a *disposition* to (1) think and (2)
think critically, and attributes such as open-mindedness, inquisitiveness,
and respect for others will come into play.

Critical thinking skills are increasingly important for learners as they
navigate each academic obstacle, and are expected to use higher-order
thinking skills more often. A good number of people learning English
are also studying other subjects *in* English (see 5), or are hoping to do
so, so courses of English for Academic Puposes (EAP) almost invariably
include training in critical approaches to reading and writing. In more
general courses, a critical-thinking strand is often added to the syllabus
in a more scattergun approach and it sometimes competes for space on
the page with other 21st century skills, such as empathy, being a positive
team member, or showing initiative.

A detailed list of the components of critical thinking is long, but it
would include concluding, evaluating, exemplifying, linking, prioritising,
specifying, and summarising. All useful tools to have!

In practice

The extent to which anyone might acquire these skills in an English
language class depends, at least in part, on how much time is devoted

to exploring and practising them. An occasional text about fake news or an opinion essay about reality TV may be the bases for some useful language practice but they won't do much, alone, to advance the cause of digital information literacy or more general critical thinking skills. The learning material that is labelled 'critical thinking' does not always differentiate between 'using critical thinking' and 'becoming a better critical thinker', and the former does not always lead to the latter. But cognitively more challenging tasks and texts may motivate and engage some (but not all!) learners and lead to extensive opportunities for authentic language practice.

Fuller approaches to critical thinking can be found in EAP courses, where critical thinking and academic language learning are seen to be mutually supportive. Training in academic writing, broken down into components like paragraph structure, ordering information, coherence, and editing, is easily combined with a critical-thinking approach to reading, where students analyse and evaluate a text.

Training in critical thinking is more likely to lead to desired outcomes if the institution is supportive, if the materials are available, if the teacher has bought into the idea, and if there is enough time to avoid a tokenistic approach. Other 21st century skills, especially creative thinking (see **9**) and digital literacy (see **10**), are not entirely dissociable from critical thinking, and commonly combine in learning materials.

Critical thinking can be integrated into language learning in a wide variety of complex ways. If, as Dummett and Hughes (2019) suggest, critical thinking can only be loosely defined as reflective, rational, and reasonable thinking, any activity which promotes the use of such thinking must surely be welcomed. This means that there are implications for the teacher's role, with probably less emphasis on the teacher's authority.

Takeaways

There is enough evidence to show that critical thinking training leads to some gains in academic work, but there is a lack of evidence to show that this is transferred to other areas of learners' lives. There's a lively debate about the extent to which critical thinking depends on knowledge of particular subjects: in order, for example, for someone to think critically about the Covid pandemic, climate change, or last night's football, they need to have some factual information before they begin. What counts as a fact is not shared by everyone, of course. But if critical thinking does not always readily lend itself to transfer from one domain of knowledge to another, how should it be assessed?

There are formal tests to assess the critical thinking and problem-solving skills of learners, such as the TSA of Cambridge Assessment. In this test, candidates must, for example, select the relevant, and ignore the irrelevant information to solve a 'real-world' problem. There are also frameworks that offer potential for self-assessment and formative feedback (such as the Cambridge Life Competencies Framework: Critical Thinking). High stakes, summative evaluations of critical thinking skills may hinder the development of the very skills they are supposed to be measuring, but the pressure to measure outcomes is hard to avoid.

A commonly discussed sub-division of critical thinking at the present time is the ability to spot fake news – 'media information literacy', to use the jargon. Lessons about fake news are now common in many ELT contexts. It's unfortunate that research into the effectiveness of promoting media information literacy has provided only mixed results.

One final thought. It's often argued that a language class is a good place for critical thinking work, but there's also a strong argument that the learners' own language might be a better starting point.

Cottrell, S. (2005). *Critical thinking skills: Developing effective analysis and argument.* Basingstoke: Palgrave Macmillan.

Dummett, P. and Hughes, J. (2019). *Critical Thinking in ELT.* Boston, MA.: National Geographic Learning.

Lai, E. R. (2011). Critical Thinking: A Literature Review (Pearson) Available online at: http://images.pearsonassessments.com/images/tmrs/CriticalThinkingReviewFINAL.pdf

9   Creative thinking

> It's easy for us all to agree that 'creative thinking' is a good thing, and that it plays an important role in the classroom. But the label covers two very different sets of priorities.

What and why?

The terms *creative thinking* and *creativity* are often used interchangeably, and there is no generally accepted definition for either of them. There are, however, two distinctly different ways in which both terms are approached. In the first of these, creative thinking comes under the umbrella of 21st century skills (see 7). It is seen as a vital component of our ability to solve technological, economic and organisational problems in a rapidly changing world. Its value, ultimately, is found in its potential to enhance the economic performance of the flexible 'creative thinker' and the organisation they work for. It is closely related to critical thinking (see 8), since problems must be critically analysed before creative solutions to them are found. This kind of creative thinking is usually indistinguishable from 'innovation skills'. Whilst its importance in education is widely accepted, the specific details of what it consists of remain a matter of debate. For example, researchers continue to discuss the extent to which creative thinking skills (along with critical thinking) can be applied to everything that a learner does, or whether they can only be transferred to specific activities.

The second type of creative thinking is less concerned with investment in human capital, and more with the expression of a learner's inner world and the potential for personal development. This development is made possible through learners' engagement with activities which often involve the arts (drama, stories, music, song, poetry, dance, etc.). It usually requires them to produce language in ways in which personalized, emotional self-expression is prioritised. Besides reflecting the inherently creative nature of language, the value of such an approach is also to be found in gains in motivation and self-esteem. In the process, it may be hoped that learners become more receptive to new ideas and ways of doing things.

In calls for more creative thinking in language teaching and learning, these different approaches are often blurred, with the result that justification for one approach may be seen as justification for the other, even though they have relatively little in common.

In practice

Creative thinking, of the 21st century variety, is a wide range of interrelated skills which, using the definition of the OECD's PISA 2021 programme, allow for the generation, evaluation and improvement of ideas that will lead to effective and original solutions to particular problems. One educational approach, *Problem-based learning* (PBL), has been widely promoted in general educational contexts as a way of developing creative thinking. In PBL, learners are presented with an open-ended real-world problem, such as finding ways of reducing the carbon footprint of the school. They work collaboratively in small groups, supported by a range of digital technologies, to define the problem clearly, organise their previous knowledge, brainstorm ideas, make hypotheses, and carry out research while moving towards tentative solutions. The approach has been tried out to a very limited extent in English language learning contexts, but has yet to gain broad acceptance. It imposes a high cognitive load on learners, and when the work has to be done in another language, there is inevitably a high linguistic load, as well. Research so far has failed to show convincing evidence that PBL results in gains in creative thinking, and this has led some scholars to conclude that getting learners to solve problems may not be the best way of learning how to solve problems.

A more piecemeal approach to developing creative thinking in English language classes breaks things down into smaller parts. Defining problems, forming hypotheses, brainstorming, etc. – the sub-skills of creative thinking – are practised in the course of other activities in much the same way as critical thinking skills are often practised (see 8) and the overlap between these two kinds of thinking makes them hard to disentangle. When viewed as a 21st century skill, training in creative thinking is also likely to be closely linked to the use of digital technologies (see **10**) which facilitate either the creative process or creative production (e.g. collaborative idea sharing, bulletin boards, vision boards, wikis, mindmap generators, video production and editing).

ELT publications, however, more often reflect the second kind of creative thinking (see the reading suggestions below). The range of possibilities is too wide to do full justice here, but the most common activities include:

- the use of visual art, music and literature as a prompt for writing or speaking
- the production of creative writing, especially poems, visual displays, artefacts (like masks or puppets) and video clips
- the performance of drama or poetry, or improvisation
- imaginative or playful manipulation of language
- visualisation activities (e.g. during a listening).

Takeaways

Attempts in the last twenty years to measure 21st century creative thinking have not been entirely satisfactory, not least because of problems in defining precisely what it is. However, the decision of the OECD to evaluate creative thinking skills in its PISA tests is likely to lead to creative thinking becoming increasingly important for language teachers, especially school teachers in OECD countries. This will probably impact most on CLIL teachers (see **4**) where the learners' creative thinking in particular academic subjects can be assessed.

The OECD has made clear that it wishes to push creative thinking up the educational agenda and assessing it is one way of doing so. As with anything that is assessed, there will be a washback effect on classroom practices. Since both definitions and ways of assessing creative thinking will probably continue to be revised for some time, the precise washback effects are also likely to evolve.

Meanwhile, the more arts-oriented variety of creative thinking, which has been around for many decades, will continue to offer language teachers a rich compendium of activities and materials they can select from. Writing poetry or performing drama will probably be appropriate more often to classes of younger learners than adults with utilitarian goals, but the very creativity of the ideas suggested by authors in the list below may provide inspiration to all teachers.

Clare, A. and Marsh, A. (2020). *The Creative Teacher's Compendium*. Shoreham-by-Sea: Pavilion Publishing.

Maley, A. (2018). *Alan Maley's 50 Creative Activities*. Cambridge: Cambridge University Press.

Maley, A. and Kiss, T. (2018). *Creativity and English Language Teaching*. London: Palgrave Macmillan.

Peachey, N. (2019). *Hacking Creativity*. PeacheyPublications.

Pugliese, C. (2010). *Being Creative*. Peaslake: DELTA.

10   Digital literacies

> There's a thin dividing line between developing digital literacies and using technology for its own sake. It's not always easy to stay on the right side of the line.

What and why?

Like the other 21st century skills discussed in this book (see **7**, **8** and **9**), there is a problem when it comes to a precise definition of digital literacies. There are well over one hundred, and still growing, different frameworks that attempt to capture the idea of digital literacies. They have much in common and, broadly speaking, concern the skills that people need, when using technology, to find, evaluate, organise and communicate information. In our increasingly digitalised world, it is generally agreed that such skills are necessary for individuals to flourish in their work, their studies and their everyday lives. As a result, it is now rare to find a national education system which does not promote the use of technology in learning, and training in the skills that are needed to make best use of it.

The number of people, of all ages, using digital tools to learn English grew rapidly in the first decades of the 21st century. Better connectivity, along with the proliferation of platforms, mobile devices, apps and learning materials, made possible the expansion of digitally supported language learning of all kinds, from institutional study through a learning platform or flipped approaches (see **12**) to more informal and self-driven forms of independent study.

With the unprecedented global shift to online activities in 2020, caused by the Covid pandemic, the importance of digital literacies in all aspects of our lives has become even more acute, not least for learners and teachers of languages. There had always been an awareness of a 'digital divide' between those with access to technology and those without. With so much learning taking place online, a divide between those with and without digital literacies has also become much more apparent.

At the most basic level, digital literacies for language learners and teachers involve the technical skills needed to operate in a digital environment. These may range from the very elementary (such as using online search or posting on social media) to more sophisticated skills (such as setting up a blog or creating and editing video). Training in digital literacies invariably entails the use of a variety of digital tools that have been designed to help users operate in a variety of ways online.

However, it has long been recognised that digital literacies are much more than just technical competences. At least as important as the tools that are used is the way in which they are used, since these tools affect how we think, communicate, relate with others, and behave. Accordingly, digital literacies are also concerned with cognitive, emotional and social practices. This has led researchers to break digital literacies down into a large number of smaller categories. These include:

- network literacy – the way in which we build and participate in digital social networks
- personal literacy – the way in which our identities are projected and protected online
- critical digital literacy (see 8) – the way in which we critically evaluate online content.

Taken together, these form what could be described as a sort of reflective competence. They underline the importance for learners to be both sceptical and proactive in their interactions with digital tools.

In practice

If teachers are to help their students with digital literacies, they must, of course, be digitally literate themselves. Specifications of the digital competences required by English language teachers have been drawn up in two frameworks (see 20): the TESOL Technology Standards Framework and the Cambridge English Digital Framework for Language Teachers, both freely available online. Although they adopt rather different approaches, both are primarily concerned with the immediate applications of technology to *learning*, rather than digital literacies outside learning contexts.

In line with these frameworks, teacher training in many parts of the world has long encouraged the use of a variety of digital tools, and sometimes compelled it. Materials to support teachers in integrating technology in their lessons are widely available, ranging from interactive tutorials and online how-to videos to books full of practical ideas (e.g. Stanley, 2013; Hockly, 2017). Reflecting the main concern of the frameworks, support for the development of learners' and teachers' digital literacies in their out-of-class lives, and which goes beyond technical competence, remains relatively rare.

One exception to this is critical digital literacy, and learning materials about fake news are now common.

Takeaways

There can be no doubt that the incorporation of various technologies in English language lessons has the *potential* to enrich the learning and teaching process. Unfortunately, there is no guarantee that it will do so, and research by the OECD (so keen to promote the use of educational technology) has not found 'appreciable improvements' in learning as a result of wider technology use. Technology can also be used for largely gratuitous purposes by teachers in the classroom, and it often is. But if most of us have, at some point, experimented with a piece of technology in our teaching for no particularly good reason, it seems unfair to blame us for it. Teachers have been encouraged, for decades, to try out new technologies, where the only likely benefit to some learners is temporarily enhanced motivation – if the affective response to the new technology is positive.

Learning activities that involve technology use and, at the same time, promote a better understanding of the way that this technology affects our social, emotional and cognitive behaviour, are hard to find, although *Digital Literacies* (Dudeney et al., 2022) has a good selection to choose from. You may prefer, like me, to write your own materials. Some of these materials and activities may lead to rich and interesting lessons, but unless they are structured and sequenced in some sensible way, there is a danger they will be a collection of one-offs.

It makes sense to incorporate digital literacies across the curriculum, with activities in the English class complementing those in other classes.

But this often presents practical problems or is simply impossible for whatever reason (e.g. a school policy banning phones). Given the importance of digital literacies, there is also a strong case for dealing with them in the learners' first language. When English classes are the only places where digital literacies are addressed, impact will be limited.

What's more, research evidence for the effectiveness of training in fake-news spotting or changing attitudes and practices concerned with online security, privacy or data abuse is, unfortunately, thin on the ground. Still, topics such as these may be relevant and interesting to some learners, and nothing is to be lost from addressing them.

Dudeney, G., Hockly, N. and Pegrum, M. (2022). *Digital Literacies 2nd edition*. Abingdon: Routledge.

Hockly, N. (2017). *ETpedia Technology*. Hove: Pavilion Publishing.

Stanley, G. (2013). *Language Learning with Technology*. Cambridge: Cambridge University Press.

11

Blended learning

> Blended learning can offer advantages to both learners and
> teachers only if a number of important conditions are met.
> When they are not, as is often the case, it is unlikely that
> the use of educational technology will add much of value
> to language teaching.

What and why?

When, in the early years of this century, the term *blended learning* first
became part of educational discourse, it referred to the combination
of learning in traditional face-to-face contexts with learning with
technology, CD-ROMs in particular. Around 2010, commentators were
already arguing that the term was redundant, as the use of technology
in language learning had already become completely normalised in
many parts of the world. Let's just talk about 'learning', they suggested,
not without good cause. Nevertheless, 'blended learning' continues to
be a buzz word, although – surprise, surprise – there are disagreements
about precisely what it is.

The technology moved on, with learning platforms and other resources
increasingly accessed by mobile devices. With the enforced switch
to online learning as a result of the Covid pandemic, the use of
technology in language learning was indisputably normalised. Blended
learning, however, has remained a hot topic because the challenges it
presented from the start have not gone away.

The use of technology to aid learning was driven primarily by more
of an interest in technology than in learning, and this remains the case
with teachers in many contexts required (or strongly encouraged) to
use it, often for reasons more related to digital literacies (see 10) than
to an understanding of how it might promote language acquisition.
Ongoing discussions about the importance of putting pedagogy before
technology reflect the common reality that is the other way round.

The roots of blended learning are to be found in the corporate world, where financial savings could be made through a reduction in the costs of face-to-face training. In language teaching, where it is unlikely that classroom time is ever sufficient to make necessary progress, homework has always been seen as an essential addition to the work of the teacher. Embracing the potential of technology, homework has become blended learning.

This potential includes the availability of a wide range of interactive materials, the scope of this material to promote greater learner autonomy, the use of technology to facilitate meaningful communication between learners, the possibility of more personalized approaches (see **18**), gains in motivation in learners who enjoy using technology, and time-saving automated feedback (see **24**).

In practice

In blended learning, the ratio of synchronous face-to-face teaching to asynchronous online work can be absolutely anything. The online work may be seen as preparatory to class sessions (see **12**) or as a follow-up to it. In course material produced by big international publishers, it was traditional homework, in the form of workbooks, that first became available in digital format. At times now, these are not even available in print format. The Covid pandemic saw publishers rushing to convert all course materials to digital format, and it is now hard to imagine any published course which cannot be blended in many different ways.

It is clear that switching from traditional to online teaching is not a simple matter and that combining synchronous and asynchronous study is as important now as it ever was. The ongoing challenge is how to optimise the blend. There is no single solution, but a number of necessary conditions have been identified.

First, both teachers and learners need to know how to make good use of the digital tools and materials. This may take some time, and training and ongoing trouble-shooting support are often needed. Second, the synchronous and asynchronous components of the blend need to be closely integrated. When, as is often the case, it is hard for learners to see the link between the two, there is a risk that they will be less engaged with the self-study and fail to give it sufficient attention. Very careful thought, therefore, needs to be given to the way that both parts of the blend are assessed, both formatively and summatively. Third, in order to engage fully with the self-study, learners will need a degree of autonomy, of self-regulation, of metacognitive awareness (see 28), and, for this, training may also be needed.

There is plenty of evidence that blended courses can be very effective, but, at the same time, there is no shortage of examples where there was much less success than hoped for. Technological problems and negative attitudes on the part of teachers and learners have sometimes proved difficult to resolve. Institutions have frequently underestimated the need for teacher training. Paradoxically, for an approach which can offer flexibility, some institutions have not always been sufficiently flexible in the way it was introduced, failing to allow for continuous review and modifications. Anticipated cost savings have often failed to materialise.

Takeaways

When technologies are used as substitutes for other tools, or when they offer only minor enhancements, learning gains will be, at best, limited. The use of digital workbooks is a case in point, although instant automatic correction and tracking of learners' work are valuable improvements. The use of educational technology encourages us to reflect on which activities are best carried out in the face-to-face classroom (i.e. those which involve social interaction) and which can be allocated to self-study (e.g. memorisation tasks and mechanical practice of language).

Technology, however, will be most transformative when it allows for significant changes in the kinds of learning tasks that are carried out. Extensive reading and listening are both qualitatively different when using personalizable online tools (e.g. hyperlinks, dictionary look-ups, captions). Online collaborative writing, using a tool like Google Docs, has much greater potential than its equivalent in the classroom. The use of video software in making presentations and in project work opens up exciting possibilities. All of these examples represent significant shifts in the ways in which language learning can be facilitated.

The inescapable conclusion, I think, is that the pre-service training and in-service support of teachers needs to focus less on learning how to use particular technologies, and more on what we know about the processes of second language acquisition, and about educational psychology. The global evidence that we have suggests, sadly, that the introduction of digital technologies rarely brings about any appreciable improvements in learning. The most likely reason for this is that educational technology is employed and promoted mostly for its own sake, and not as a solution to a specific educational question.

McCarthy, M. (Ed.) (2016). *The Cambridge Guide to Blended Learning for Language Teaching*. Cambridge: Cambridge University Press.

Russell, V. and Murphy-Judy, K. (2021). *Teaching language online: A guide to designing, developing, and delivering online, blended, and flipped language courses*. New York: Routledge.

Sharma, P. and Barrett, B. (2009). *Blended Learning: Using Technology in and Beyond the Language Classroom*. Oxford: Macmillan.

12

Flipped learning

Flipped learning is a form of blended learning (see 11)
which is rich in promise. The challenges, however, should
not be underestimated, and it may not be feasible in many
contexts.

What and why?

The basic idea behind flipped learning is deceptively simple: work that
was 'traditionally done in the class is now done at home, and what was
traditionally homework is now completed in class' (Bergmann and Sams,
2012: 13). Although not entirely new, the idea acquired a name at the start
of the 21st century and rapidly gained in popularity after a TED talk by
Sal Khan, the founder of Khan Academy, in 2011. The Khan Academy,
funded by technology companies (like Google) and technology-associated
foundations (like the Bill and Melinda Gates Foundation), produces
educational videos, mostly with a focus on science and technology subjects.

Within a few years, English language educators had enthusiastically
picked up on the idea. The appeal lay in its potential to free up classroom
time for communication between learners by assigning more formal study
(especially of grammar) as homework tasks. Many teachers had been
trying to do precisely this for at least decades, using self-study grammar
books and vocabulary lists, but technology, in the form of video, ebooks
and platforms made the shift a more attractive proposition.

There are a number of other reasons why flipped learning appears to
offer a new and improved learning paradigm. Most importantly, a greater
degree of personalization is possible when learners are studying in their
own time (see **18**). Learners no longer need to be following exactly the
same materials or the same sequence of activities. Other reasons include:

- It is much easier to cater to learners with specific learning needs
  (e.g. materials designed for dyslexics or text-to-speech software
  for the blind and partially sighted, see **6**).

- It is also easier to cater to the needs of learners with different levels of proficiency or with different interests.
- It allows learners to proceed at their own pace, taking more or less time to consult reference sources, and repeating exercises when desired or necessary.

When the self-study takes place with materials delivered on a sophisticated learning platform (as opposed to a simple platform where documents can just be shared), other potential advantages may also accrue.

- Corrective feedback on learners' work can be both automatic (see 24) and formative, offering suggestions about what to do next.
- Interaction (outside the face-to-face classroom) between learners when engaged in collaborative work is possible.
- Teachers may be able to provide learners with more individualised support.

In practice

It is probably now the case that most flipped approaches in English language teaching involve online study using platform-delivered materials. Both grammar and vocabulary instruction are often flipped, making use of the interactive practice opportunities of digital materials. A strong argument can also be made for flipping listening and extensive reading tasks. Most students are likely to benefit from the technological possibilities of doing these things online: these include better sound quality, the use of pause/repeat, speech-to-text software, and automated dictionary look-up. Neither activity, in any case, makes the most of the communicative possibilities of the face-to-face classroom.

Whichever aspect of the curriculum is flipped, there is likely to be a reorientation of the teacher's role in the learning process if the teacher's explanatory function has been reduced by shifting the more formal study online. This has been popularly described as a move from the teacher as 'sage on the stage' to the 'guide on the side'. For flipped learning to be effective, it will almost certainly entail more work for the teacher. Planning and monitoring learners' personalized self-study and using the insights gained from this to inform the planning and running of face-to-face classes requires hard work.

During both the self-study and the face-to-face classes, the teacher's role as a motivator, manager and supporter will take precedence over the more traditional roles of instructor and provider of models. With this move towards a more learner-centred approach, feedback will need to be both more personalized and more formative. Some teachers will need support themselves as they transition to these new roles.

Takeaways

For all the potential of flipped learning, it is disappointing to learn that research findings are not more positive. Meta-analyses (see 30) of flipped learning in general educational contexts have not found that the approach leads to significant learning gains. More disappointing still is the fact (a) that the learning gains that were found were only short-term, and (b) that flipped learning led to a widening of the achievement gap between stronger and weaker students. In ELT contexts, very little robust research exists and accounts of flipped learning show more enthusiasm than empirical evidence. Why might this be?

Flipped learning can only fulfil its potential if learners actually do the work that has been flipped. Unfortunately, this cannot be counted on. According to one estimate, only about three-quarters of learners complete out-of-class assignments regularly. The challenge of getting learners to do homework does not diminish when this work takes place online. If anything, it increases.

The main reason for this is that learners who must complete a substantial portion of their work individually need to be effective self-regulators (see 28). This is more likely to be the case in higher education when they have already, by definition, demonstrated some success in learning. In the absence of self-regulation strategies, learners will need considerable support and training. Flipped learning, then, is best introduced gradually and experimentally, and teacher support for learners during self-study time may be imperative.

The challenges of motivation and self-regulation may also be exacerbated by two other issues. The first of these is technological: access to a suitable device with good data connections cannot be taken for granted. The second is a problem of attitudes: learners used to more traditional teacher-centred instruction may find it difficult to adjust.

Negative attitudes may also be compounded by the perception, at least at first, that their workload is greater than before.

Flipped learning clearly has much to offer, but, sadly, not for everyone. It is, for example, highly unlikely to prove effective with learners lacking the intellectual maturity that is required, or with those whose levels of motivation are insufficiently high. It also requires buy-in from both teachers and institutions, and continuing levels of training and technological support will be required.

Bauer-Ramazani, C., Graney, J. M., Marshall, H. W. and Sabieh, C. (2016). Flipped Learning in TESOL: Definitions, Approaches, and Implementation. *TESOL Journal* 7 (2): 429–437.

Bergmann, J. and Sams, A. (2012). *Flip Your Classroom: Reach every student in every class every day*. Washington, D.C.: International Society for Technology in Education.

Brinks Lockwood, R. (2014). *Flip It! Strategies for the ESL Classroom*. Ann Arbor: University of Michigan Press.

Voss, E. and Kostka, I. (2019). *Flipping Academic English Language Learning: Experiences from an American University*. Berlin: Springer.

13 Engagement

> All teachers have experience of bored, disengaged students, and addressing the problem is one of the greatest challenges that we face. There are things that can be done, but solutions are multi-dimensional, complex and with no guarantee of success.

What and why?

When learners are not actively participating and engaged in a class activity, it is unlikely that much, if any, of the intended learning will actually take place. Either as students or as teachers, it is a situation which we have undoubtedly experienced. A lack of engagement may be observed in learners' behaviour – slowness to follow a teacher's instructions, failure to ask questions, minimal participation or collaboration with peers, overfast task completion, and even disruption – although all of these may also have other causes. Low levels of engagement are not always easy to observe, not least because some students, particularly in compulsory education settings, have learnt to simulate attention and interest. Two aspects of engagement are necessary for language learning to occur. The first of these is cognitive engagement, or the degree to which learners are attentive and are thinking about the task at hand. This may be observed, for example, in the extent to which learners self-correct or how they work with others to find appropriate ways to express meaning. Closely related is social and emotional engagement. This may be seen in active listening, sharing ideas and language from peers, giving and accepting peer feedback, and in showing enjoyment, enthusiasm and curiosity. Engagement is multidimensional in nature – a complex behavioural, cognitive and social-emotional web.

Keeping students engaged is clearly more of a challenge in learning online with a video platform, where it is harder to sustain learners' interest. There are few teachers who have not struggled to deal with the phenomenon of 'zoomed out' learners. Body language and eye contact provide a teacher with important clues to a learner's level of engagement, but these clues are often not available in online lessons, so identifying a lack of engagement may not be easy. The shift to online teaching has brought the importance of engagement into sharper focus.

For an issue of such importance, it is surprising that engagement has not attracted the interest of language learning researchers until recently. At first, researchers focussed primarily on ways of promoting engagement during communicative speaking tasks. Interest has now widened to include all aspects of language teaching (Mercer and Dörnyei, 2020).

In practice

No learning task can be considered intrinsically engaging, as the level of engagement that a task will generate will depend on the interplay of many factors. These include task design, the way that a task is managed in the classroom, and the motivational 'baggage' that learners bring to learning activities, as well as wider contextual issues over which a teacher may have little control. For the first three of these factors, it is possible to identify principles that will contribute to engagement.

Task design

Engaging tasks involve materials and activities that learners see as interesting, authentic, and relevant, both to them personally and to their lives outside the classroom. They involve a degree of cognitive challenge, but not to the extent that the task is seen as undoable. Familiarity with task and topic often generate more positive responses, but elements of surprise may play a positive role. The language requirements of the task must be within the learners' abilities, but some 'stretching' will be necessary for more learning opportunities. Tasks which require some kind of individualised input from learners (the sharing of personal experiences or learner-driven research, for example) will often be more motivating. Finally, learners will benefit from being able to feel a sense of achievement when the task has been completed.

Task management

There needs to be a positive emotional response to a task, and this is more likely when there are plenty of opportunities to collaborate with peers. This is why the use of break-out rooms is so important in online lessons. There also needs to be a strong sense of group cohesiveness, and this will usually need to be developed over weeks and months. Learners often demonstrate more engagement when they have a feeling of control over learning tasks and the way they carry them out. Offering learners a choice of tasks or a choice in the way they approach them may, therefore, lead to greater motivation.

Positive emotional responses will not be helped by feelings of anxiety, and the teacher's role is likely to be critical in this respect. An approachable manner, sensitive listening skills, a ready responsiveness to individual concerns, and a genuine interest in the learners will all contribute. Mercer and Dörnyei (2020) recommend that teachers think and behave like a coach (see **29**), prioritising dialogue with learners over telling them what to do, in order to encourage them to take responsibility for their learning.

Dealing with motivational 'baggage'

According to one of the oldest English proverbs, you can lead a horse to water, but you cannot make it drink. Learners are unlikely to engage in learning activities unless they are willing to do so, and nurturing this willingness can be a major challenge. Learners need to have a positive attitude towards English and they need to believe that they can learn it, so that it is worth the effort that the learning requires. Educational psychologists consequently advise teachers to promote a 'growth mindset' (see **14**) in their learners. Since learning a language requires long-term engagement, teachers are also advised to develop their learners' perseverance and resilience, also known as *grit* (see **15**).

Takeaways

This list of tips is already long, but could easily be extended if I had more space. Unfortunately, there is no guarantee that following the advice will lead to learner engagement. Some interventions are unpredictable in their outcomes (for example, providing choice may result in more enjoyment, but greater anxiety). For others, like promoting growth mindsets and grit, there is little reliable evidence of their efficacy. This is not to say that the advice is not useful, but it is important to remember that there are limits to how much individual teachers can affect their students' learning.

Attitudes towards learning English will be significantly shaped by broader institutional issues outside most teachers' control. These include tiredness caused by timetabling issues and the importance that is attached to the testing of English (especially speaking skills), as well as a school's behavioural management policies, its emotional climate and general ethos. To the list of advice, therefore, we need to add consideration of how teachers can best work with their colleagues to influence whole-school culture so that their own interventions to improve engagement have maximum impact.

Hendra, L. A. and Jones, C. (2018). *Motivating learners with immersive speaking tasks: Part of the Cambridge Papers in ELT series.* [pdf] Cambridge: Cambridge University Press.

Hiver, P., Al-Hoorie, A. H. and Mercer, S. (Eds.) (2020). *Student Engagement in the Language Classroom.* Bristol, UK: Multilingual Matters.

Mercer, S. and Dörnyei, Z. (2020). *Engaging Language Learners in Contemporary Classrooms.* Cambridge: Cambridge University Press.

Nakamura, S., Phung L. and Reinders, H. (2021). The effect of learner choice on L2 task engagement. *Studies in Second Language Acquisition*, 43 (2): 428–441.

Mindsets

A belief in one's ability to succeed through effort can have a significant influence on one's chances of success. Promoting such self-belief in learners is an important part of a teacher's job, but also one of our most difficult challenges.

What and why?

Mindsets are beliefs about one's abilities. According to Carol Dweck (2006), the founder of mindset theory, people can be placed on a continuum with, at one end, those who believe that their abilities (such as intelligence) can be developed (growth mindset), and, at the other, those who believe that their abilities are fixed and cannot be improved (fixed mindset). These beliefs often vary, from one kind of ability to another, so that one person might have a fixed mindset about, say, musical ability, and a growth mindset about, say, sport. Language learners typically hold beliefs about their ability to learn a language at some point on the continuum between fixed and growth, and these may be broken down into beliefs about particular aspects of language learning. For example, a learner may have a fixed mindset about pronunciation, but a growth mindset about vocabulary development (Mercer and Ryan, 2010).

It is said that students with growth mindsets work hard to make progress without needing the rewards that are provided by positive evaluations of their performance (in the form of tests, for example). Growth mindsets correlate with increased motivation, engagement (see **13**) and grit (see **15**). This ought to mean that they also correlate with better academic achievement, but opinions here are divided and studies show the correlation between the two may sometimes be only weak. There is, however, evidence of a stronger correlation for disadvantaged students (for example, those with low socio-economic status).

Despite questions about the connections between mindset and achievement, the belief that growth mindset can and should be taught has become orthodox. The idea that teachers should encourage their students to believe that they can succeed through hard work sounds like basic common sense. According to one recent report, 98 percent of teachers in the US believe that adopting growth mindset approaches in the classroom will lead to improved learning. The view is shared and supported by many national educational authorities and influential organisations like the World Bank. Generous funding has fuelled the enthusiasm of teachers, and growth mindset applications and research have now become a multi-million dollar mini-industry.

In practice

Since mindsets are typically implicit, they can only be changed when they are made explicit. One of the most common approaches to developing growth mindset is to teach learners about the functioning of the brain in direct ways, through texts, videos and workshops, with a focus on the brain's plasticity, so that they can better understand the value of effort. After blocks of study, learners can be encouraged to positively self-evaluate by completing 'now-I-can' reflection tasks.

A second common approach is to teach through examples, in which learners explore the biographies of people, who have overcome failure and achieved success, often despite adversity. These role models may include teachers themselves, whose own stories of difficulties, but ultimately success, in learning English, may act as inspiration.

Motivational classroom posters with inspirational quotes of the 'yes-you-can' variety are often used as reminders of the importance of positive self-belief. Teacher feedback on learners' work is upbeat, focussing on the future: even if learning challenges have not yet been resolved, mistakes are opportunities to learn. Teachers' generous praise – of effort, not ability – is believed to reinforce the message. For out of class, there is a wide range of growth mindset apps that can be bought, including one, *Brainology*, developed by Carol Dweck.

The belief that, little by little, learners can acquire a growth mindset in the ways suggested above is widespread, but research evidence is sadly lacking. None of these ideas is likely to take up too much time or cause any harm, and some may be valuable, irrespective of their impact on mindset. But researchers now agree that changing mindsets requires more than the occasional activity in class. The central problem is that most educational systems are structured around formal assessments of performance, which clearly do not encourage learners to see mistakes as opportunities to learn. High-stakes assessments almost inevitably undermine any attempted message to learners that they can succeed if they just try hard enough. It is not surprising that students who fail a standardised test and, as a result, have to repeat a year or join a technical school (rather than a general school), show less growth mindset than their more successful peers. This is probably both a cause and an effect of their test results.

The everyday practices of teachers probably have more impact on mindsets than specifically mindset-oriented activities. According to a recent large-scale report (OECD, 2021), the greatest impacts on growth mindset come when students perceive their teachers as being supportive in a safe learning environment, and when teachers adapt their teaching to the needs of the class, as opposed to simply following a fixed syllabus.

Takeaways

Mindset theory is still relatively young and research is ongoing, but it is already clear that the early enthusiasm for mindset interventions was often misguided. They appear to work better for some kinds of students in some kinds of schools, but they are certainly no magic bullet.

Because communicative language classrooms require learners to 'perform' their learning in a public way (in speaking activities), a growth mindset may be more important than in other school subjects. Without it, learners are unlikely to engage in activities beyond the bare minimum or to take the kinds of risks that are necessary for their language skills to develop. But recognising the importance of an attribute such as growth mindset does not mean we should assume that there are easy ways of developing it. Classrooms are complex, dynamic places with very many different factors influencing the learning that does (or does not) take place. Mindsets, too, are complex and dynamic systems: they both affect and are affected by classroom environments.

Even if teachers have not (yet) found a solution to complex mindset problems in their classes, their only chance of doing so is probably by first developing a growth mindset themselves. Dweck has argued that we need to approach mindset interventions in an experimental or exploratory manner, and reflect deeply on the conditions in our contexts that are likely to lead to positive impact. These conditions may include changes to other teaching practices, such as an increased focus on metacognitive skills (see 28), and will almost certainly entail changes to the way learners are assessed (see 20).

Burgoyne, A. P., Hambrick, D. Z. and Macnamara, B. N. (2020). How Firm Are the Foundations of Mind-Set Theory? The Claims Appear Stronger Than the Evidence. *Psychological Science*, 31(3): 258–267. https://doi.org/10.1177/0956797619897588

Dweck, C. S. (2006). *Mindset: The New Psychology of Success*. New York: Ballantine Books.

Mercer, S. and Ryan, S. (2010). A mindset for EFL: learners' beliefs about the role of natural talent. *ELT Journal*, 64 (4): 436–444.

OECD (2021). *Sky's the Limit: Growth Mindset, Students, and Schools in PISA*. https://www.oecd.org/pisa/growth-mindset.pdf

15 Grit

There is no denying the importance of emotional behaviour in learning. A focus on grit appears, at first glance, to be an obvious way of shaping more positive attitudes and better learning. A closer look at grit reveals a picture that is rather more complicated.

What and why?

Learning a language takes time. Estimates vary, but, as a minimum, something in the region of 600 hours of English language lessons (plus self-study) are probably needed to reach a functional B2 level. Without *grit* – perseverance and passion for long-term goals, regardless of rewards and recognition – learners are unlikely to carry out the work that is needed to achieve such a level. Given the importance of grit for success in both academic study and for life beyond, it is not surprising that education authorities have paid substantial attention to aspects of character education that can promote it. Supported by international bodies like the OECD and the World Bank, national governments in many countries have, in recent years, invested millions in researching and promoting grit and other non-cognitive skills, in the hope of boosting academic performance.

Non-cognitive skills, including resilience, self-control, and conscientiousness, are all closely related to grit and have long been seen as important components of effective learning. Grit itself became one of the most important areas of interest in social-emotional learning following a TED talk by Angela Duckworth in 2013 (over 26 million views at the time of writing) and the publication of her best-selling book a few years later. As the title of Duckworth's book indicates, grit has two main components. The first of these, *passion*, is described more technically as 'consistency of interest', the ability to maintain interest in a personal goal over a long period of time even when there are setbacks along the way. The second, *perseverance*, is shorthand for 'perseverance of effort', the ability, over time, to work hard – again despite challenges and difficulties. It is perseverance, not passion, that has been found to be most important in terms of improved learning outcomes.

Grit is a description of a behaviour that is likely to need a growth mindset, a positive attitude, (see **14**) behind it. It seems reasonable to assume that people with growth mindsets are much more likely to show grit, and researchers have found a correlation between growth mindsets and perseverance (but not passion). The connection between grit and growth mindset is so close that they are often conflated.

In practice

Grit may develop (or decrease) over time, but the practical challenge is to find an answer to the question of how teachers and schools can promote it. Teaching passion is a very complex undertaking, if indeed, it can be taught at all. Practical suggestions, therefore, tend to focus on perseverance of effort, and the most widely-accepted way of promoting this is by encouraging growth mindsets. Unfortunately, as we saw in the last chapter, growth mindset interventions do not have a strong track record of success. In fact, there are no evidence-based ways of improving grit in language learners (Credé, 2018) and even grit enthusiasts are unable to recommend any particular approach (Teimouri et al., 2020). While expressing the hope that grit can be learnt, even Angela Duckworth has acknowledged that we lack any proof that this is the case.

One of the most well-known approaches to behavioural management in schools is the ClassDojo app, which claims to have 35 million users from pre-school to final grade of high school in 180 countries around the world. One of the aims of ClassDojo is to promote character development and it attempts this by getting teachers to award points to individual learners for a variety of positive class values, which include 'perseverance', 'working hard', and 'participating', along with 'team work', 'helping others', and 'being on task'. Undesirable behaviour, such as being unprepared or failing to do homework, can also be awarded (negative) points. Parents can get immediate feedback as points are awarded. Its popularity alone is indication that the app goes, at least some way, towards meeting the needs of some teachers, schools and students. However, behavioural changes that result from the use of ClassDojo come at a cost. Its gamified and competitive system of rewards, based on surveillance and control, may do little to impact on long-term, intrinsic motivation. It may also negatively impact on children who, for reasons outside their control, are unable to conform to the standards expected of them. There are also concerns about such surveillance and children's right to privacy.

In more formal ways, many schools are now coming under increasing pressure to measure grit in their students. There is even a tool now available for measuring the grit of language teachers (Teimouri et al., 2020). But if grit cannot be taught, it is unclear why time should be spent in measuring it. Duckworth has observed that it is inappropriate to measure character and attempt to use this measure to judge the effectiveness of teaching. If, in addition, grit is essentially the perseverance of effort, its measurement will only tell us something that we already know: learning takes time and effort.

Takeaways

Like a number of other topics in this section of the book, such as critical and creative thinking, grit makes intuitive sense as a desirable goal. But, like them, it is not easily defined, and is best thought of as a combination of things, some of which may be impacted by teaching interventions, and some of which may not. The term *grit* has become a part of the language we use to talk about learning, but the interests of learners might be better served if we put it aside. This is not to say that perseverance of effort is not of crucial importance, but this is stale news. We have long known that a key role of teachers is to motivate learners to persevere in their efforts, and there is no shortage of well-researched ideas for how to go about this (see, for example, Dörnyei and Csizér, 1998). Teachers need, for example, to make their classes interesting, personalize their approach, build good relationships with their students, and create a positive learning environment. Learners need to be helped to focus on achievable goals and to develop autonomy and self-confidence. A focus on grit seems to add little to what we already know.

Credé, M. (2018). What shall we do about grit? A critical review of what we know and what we don't know. *Educational Researcher*: 47(9), 606–611.

Dörnyei, Z. and Csizér, K. (1998). Ten commandments for motivating language learners: results of an empirical study. *Language Teaching Research*, 2(3): 203–229.

Duckworth, A. (2016). *Grit: The Power of Passion and Perseverance*. New York: Scribner.

Teimouri, Y., Plonsky, L. and Tabandeh, F. (2020). L2 Grit: Passion and perseverance for second-language learning. *Language Teaching Research*. DOI: https://doi.org/10.1177/1362168820921895

Williamson, B. (2017). Decoding ClassDojo: psycho-policy, social-emotional learning and persuasive educational technologies. *Learning, Media and Technology*, 42 (4): pp. 440–453, DOI: 10.1080/17439884.2017.1278020

The meditative practice of mindfulness has been enthusiastically embraced by many schools and teachers as a way of improving students' behaviour and academic performance. There have certainly been some successes, but there are also reasons to be cautious about using these techniques.

What and why?

In the context of education, mindfulness most often refers to (1) a mental state of heightened and non-judgemental awareness of the present moment, and/or (2) a range of activities, which are typically of a meditative nature, intended to bring about a state of mindfulness. Attempts to provide a more specific definition of mindfulness quickly run into difficulties. There are many different tools for measuring the state of mindfulness and they evaluate slightly different things. As a consequence, what constitutes a mindfulness activity is also open to interpretation.

Inspired originally by ancient Buddhist meditational practices, mindfulness has evolved into a multi-billion dollar industry with products ranging from books, courses and apps, to essential oils, Mandala colouring sets and even a meditation Barbie. There is no generally accepted technical definition of mindfulness, and it has been criticised for being both too close to religious practices and too removed from them (Purser, 2019).

Mindfulness-based approaches have been adopted in a wide variety of settings as a way of reducing anxiety, stress, depression and pain. The corporate world has turned to mindfulness in order to improve the 'mental fitness', and therefore productivity, of employees. Google and Intel are just two of the more well-known companies to invest in mindfulness training. Its popularity has also spread rapidly to schools around the world. In the UK, for example, the 'Mindfulness in Schools Project' has already trained thousands of teachers. The benefits for students are believed to include improvements in:

- wellbeing and mental health
- concentration, working memory and planning skills
- self-esteem and awareness of social relationships
- emotional self-regulation and classroom behaviour
- academic achievement.

The benefits for teachers are thought to include general wellbeing, stress regulation and better teaching.

In practice

Mindfulness activities in the classroom often begin with a focus on developing awareness of one's body and breathing. This may involve closing the eyes and concentrating attention on different parts of the body or counting breaths. Most mindfulness manuals also recommend exercises that promote a non-judgemental, meditative exploration of the five senses. Common approaches include the contemplation of familiar objects, such as a raisin, which can be explored visually (in close-up or with light illuminating it in different ways), and through smell and taste. A third common category of activity involves the channelling of positive feelings, towards oneself and others, often by repeating a short phrase.

In addition to general techniques, such as those described above, which are often used as a warm-up for other classroom work, activities may also be more specifically related to study. Stella Cottrell's (2018) handbook of mindfulness exercises for students includes reflection on when it is hard to concentrate, highlighting positive feelings and exploring negativity about study, managing distractions, becoming a more attentive reader and listener, focusing on single tasks, developing language awareness, managing emotional blocks in writing, and regulating emotional responses to feedback from teachers.

It is hard to take issue with any of the goals of mindfulness activities, either of the general or of the more specifically study-oriented kind. Many teachers and schools are enthusiastic, but what is known about the effectiveness of these techniques? There has been no shortage of research into mindfulness in recent years, but much of it, unfortunately, has been of low quality (Van Dam et al., 2018). It has suffered from poor experimental design, a failure to use randomised control groups, undisclosed conflicts of interest on the part of researchers, and publication bias (the tendency not to report negative findings). Nevertheless, it is possible to say that mindfulness can lead to improvements in physical and mental health, and cognitive performance. Like so many of the trends described in this section of the book, it might, as the 'Mindfulness in Schools Project' concluded, be 'worth trying'. We do not, however, know what kind of mindfulness activities are most effective, for how long and how often they should be carried out, or whether teachers need special training. In short, there is more that we do not know than we know. Some reviews of the evidence have not found any impact on behaviour or academic achievement. Mindfulness programmes clearly do not work for everyone, everywhere.

Takeaways

Mindfulness cannot be forced. Compulsion would undermine the process from the start. Students (and teachers) need to 'be open to the experience and commit to giving it a go' (Cottrell, 2018), and, for many, this will require a certain leap of faith. Without respect for and trust in the teacher, students cannot be expected to show an open-minded commitment to mindfulness in the classroom. Building trust, a key condition in communicative language classrooms, is essential for the success of a wide variety of learning activities, but is not easily achieved in many contexts. It may, for example, be harder to win the trust of adolescents than that of younger learners. It probably makes sense to wait until there is enough trust before diving into mindfulness techniques.

Even when mindfulness programmes are shown to have a positive impact, we cannot usually say which aspects of these programmes were beneficial. Breathing exercises, which are not necessarily connected to mindfulness, may have a value in breaking up classroom routines, allowing better subsequent engagement and attention. The same is almost certainly true of bursts of physical activity, which are clearly not part of a mindfulness approach, and some research suggests that these may be just as beneficial as meditative techniques. According to mindfulness experts, the common response of 'zoning out' during meditation is not a mindful experience, but it may be precisely the rest that comes from zoning out that some students need and find helpful. There are, in short, many familiar ways in which teachers can try to alleviate stress and anxiety in their students. Mindfulness may not be needed at all.

It is said that mindfulness works best, on a personal level, when there are no predetermined goals, when practitioners are simply open to possibilities. Mindfulness, however, is usually introduced by teachers and schools with very clear goals in mind. Rather than assuming that mindfulness will help to achieve those goals, it might be wiser to concentrate on what we already know about how trust, engagement (see **13**), positive attitudes (see **14**) and effort (see **15**) may be promoted.

Cottrell, S. (2018). *Mindfulness for Students*. London: Macmillan.

Purser, R. E. (2019). *McMindfulness*. London: Repeater Books.

Van Dam, N. T., van Vugt, M. K., Vago, D. R., Schmalzl, L., Saron, C. D., Olendzki, A., Meissner, T., Lazar, S. W., Gorchov, J., Fox, K. C. R., Field, B. A., Britton, W., Brefczynski-Lewis, J. A. and Meyer, D. E. (2018). Mind the Hype: A Critical Evaluation and Prescriptive Agenda for Research on Mindfulness and Meditation. *Perspectives on Psychological Science* 13: pp. 36–61.

C: Rethinking teaching

Global educational policies in recent years have brought two main concerns into the spotlight: the importance of educational technology and the need to measure learning and teaching. Both are supported by a network of national and international organisations in the hope of making education more relevant to our contemporary world and more efficient at the same time. The two are closely interlinked since technology allows assessment in ways that were previously unimaginable. Current educational policies often also highlight the idea of 'lifelong learning'. Such an objective requires learners to be autonomous and self-regulating, especially when the learning mostly takes place online. All of these areas of interest are having a marked impact on English language teaching – and on teachers!

Teacher wellbeing matters not just for teachers themselves, but also for their learners and the institutions they work for. Although often cast as an individual matter, effective approaches to wellbeing are most likely to be collective and collaborative in nature.

What and why?

In most countries around the world, report after report finds that teaching is one of the most stressful professions. A 2020 report in the UK, for example, found that one in twenty teachers are suffering from long-term mental health problems, and this figure is rising. Sleeping problems, panic attacks, depression and burnout are common, as are associated psychosomatic disorders, especially hypertension.

The reasons are many and interrelated, and include workload and time pressure, dealing with unmotivated and ill-disciplined learners, aggression from both students and parents, constant changes to educational practices and a lack of any say in deciding these changes, constant evaluation, conflict with management and colleagues. These issues are compounded in many contexts by low salaries and low status. In many countries, teacher-bashing, when teachers are blamed for political shortcomings in the educational system, has reached unprecedented levels. A terrible catalogue of more extreme attacks (such as arrest and imprisonment) on teachers and their unions can be found on the pages of the website of Education International, a global federation of teachers' trade unions.

Many English language teachers work outside the K12 state sector, in private language schools, for example, where hourly wages are low, permanent contracts and job security are rare, and meeting the everyday needs of food and accommodation is a struggle.

The wellbeing of teachers is clearly a matter of major concern, and the Covid pandemic made things worse. Workloads typically increased as teachers had to adapt rapidly to working online, working in isolation without the support of colleagues, whilst dealing with heightened anxieties.

It is not a coincidence that recent concern about teacher wellbeing has developed at the same time as the growing interest in measuring educational outcomes (see 20). The realisation (by organisations like the World Bank and the OECD, as well as national governments) that the success of learners is closely related to the quality of their teachers has pushed the issue of teacher wellbeing high up the agenda. Measures are urgently needed to address teacher stress and burnout, and the corollary problems of teacher recruitment, sick leave, and teachers leaving the profession.

The kinds of measures that will be taken will depend on how teacher wellbeing is defined, and there is little agreement about this. One frequent categorisation differentiates external (or objective) wellbeing from internal (or subjective) wellbeing. The former is related to many of the causes of teacher stress discussed above: pay, contracts, working environment, safety, etc. The latter is a psychological construct concerned with, for example, positive relationships, a sense of meaning and purpose, autonomy, personal growth, and happiness. Whether we are talking about external or internal wellbeing, or a mixture of the two, a useful way of visualising wellbeing is to imagine it as a healthy balance between the physical, social and psychological challenges that we face in our lives and the resources that we have available to deal with them.

In practice

Addressing the external causes of issues which negatively impact on teacher wellbeing is a central concern of teachers' unions, and during the Covid pandemic this protective role was of enormous importance in many countries. The power of trades unions in an increasingly privatised world of education is, however, often limited.

As a complement and, sometimes, as an alternative to collective union pressure, others have advocated an approach that focusses more on the psychological resources that teachers can draw on to help deal with the underlying causes of the difficulties they face. It is an approach that is more concerned with positive personal growth, and less with repairing the damage caused by external factors. The only book-length treatment of teacher wellbeing in ELT (Mercer and Gregersen, 2020) adopts this line, drawing on the field of 'positive psychology', inspired by the work of Martin Seligman. Placing individual teachers as the focus of attention, the practical suggestions in this book encourage positive relationships with colleagues, highlighting the rewarding and enjoyable aspects of one's work, a growth mindset (see **14**), emotional self-management, an awareness of the importance of physical health, and efficient time management.

As a response to evidence that coordinated institutional approaches to the wellbeing of both learners and teachers can have a significant impact on the achievement of the former and the productivity of the latter, we are beginning to see the introduction of whole-school wellbeing policies. In some countries, including Australia and Ireland, these are supported by national ministries of education. Institutional wellbeing programmes involve mission statements, strategic prioritisation of wellbeing issues that have been identified, the creation of project teams, staff development meetings and activities that will promote a caring and collaborative community, and continuous review of the policies.

Takeaways

When problems with teacher wellbeing are serious and widespread, both the causes and solutions are likely to be structural and systemic. Without collective action to push for policy changes, often supported by unions, positive change is unlikely.

But in less extreme cases or as a preventative measure, what can individual teachers do to enhance their own wellbeing and that of their colleagues? Can the ideas drawn from positive psychology play a useful role? There are plenty of personal accounts of teachers' experiences that testify to the value of the kinds of self-help approaches that positive psychology promotes. At the same time, there is a distinct lack of robust research evidence in support of them. My own scepticism is apparent in earlier chapters about mindfulness and growth mindsets, but there can be little harm in trying things out.

Mercer and Gregersen set the tone of their book by entitling the first chapter 'It's all about me', but the rest of the book makes it clear that many of the ways in which personal wellbeing can be enhanced is by addressing the issues with colleagues, by sharing and caring with others. Collective responses to both systemic and individual issues are usually more powerful than teachers trying to work alone.

Bache, I. and Reardon, L. (2016). *The Politics and Policy of Wellbeing: Understanding the Rise and Significance of a New Agenda*. Cheltenham: Edward Elgar.

Ereaut, G. and Whiting, R. (2008). *What do we mean by 'wellbeing'? And why might it matter?* Research Report No DCSF-RW073 Department for Children, Schools and Families. https://dera.ioe.ac.uk/8572/1/dcsf-rw073%20v2.pdf

McCallum, F., Price, D., Graham, A. and Morrison, A. (2017). *Teacher wellbeing: a review of the literature*. Association of Independent Schools, NSW, Australia.

Mercer, S. and Gregersen, T. (2020). *Teacher Wellbeing*. Oxford: Oxford University Press.

Walsh, P. (2019). Precarity. *ELT Journal*, 73 (4): pp. 459–462.

Personalized learning

> We can probably all agree that depersonalized learning
> is not the best way forward, but what exactly does
> personalized learning have to offer? It depends who
> you talk to.

What and why?

Personalized learning, differentiated learning, individualised instruction, personalization … we could add to this list of near-equivalent terms without too much difficulty. There are times when they are more or less interchangeable, and there is no consensus on how to differentiate them. But of all these terms, it is *personalized learning* that is the most widely used. It is often associated with technology, as in the 2017 United States National Education Technology Plan, and concerns the ways in which learning objectives, the rate of learning and the instructional approach may be modified (usually but not necessarily by technology) to suit the needs and interests of the learner.

Personalized learning has become a rallying call for those who want to get away from the bad old days of rigid schools and teacher-fronted classrooms. It suggests more choice, freedom and autonomy, as well as greater efficacy. It can also lay claim to being a more inclusive approach (see **6**) than the enforced one-size-fits-all regimentation of traditional schooling.

Before looking at how personalized learning works out in practice, two rather different meanings of the term must be mentioned. The first of these is what we might call *personalized language practice*. As a coursebook writer, I have written a lot of material of this kind: 'Complete a sentence so that it is true for you.'

The second is a more broadly humanistic orientation to language teaching, and it dates back to the 1970s when the world of language teaching began to take an interest in individual learner differences.

'Each learner is unique in personality, abilities, and needs. Education must be personalized to fit the individual; the individual must not be dehumanized in order to meet the needs of an impersonal school system,' wrote Renée Disick in 1975. In this tradition, personalization of learning is enacted through activities which prioritise the personal experiences, thoughts and feelings of the learner. Both of these personalized learnings are interesting to explore further, but neither could really be considered a current trend.

In practice

It is invariably certain aspects of learning that are personalized, rather than the totality of the learning process. On a continuum of personalization, writing sentences that are true for you is trivial compared to learners taking control of their own learning objectives. But in schools and colleges with assigned curricula and standardised high-stakes tests, very few learners have any meaningful say in what they are studying or how they will be assessed at the end of it. Instead, they may be offered differentiated *routes* to the common objective. Unit 7 of a course can be done before Unit 4, for example. Activities can be skipped if they are not considered necessary, or repeated. Extra practice is available. This kind of personalization is at a very granular level. The freedoms it offers are very limited but usually welcome nevertheless.

Encouraging learners to study at their own rate seems like an intuitively good idea. Why force fast learners to go at the pace of their slower colleagues, and vice versa? It's not surprising that there is a long history of attempts to put such an intuitively good idea into practice. These date back, over a century ago, to a series of initiatives in the United States, which allowed students to progress through materials at their own pace, aided by technology of one kind or another. Standardised tests were just one of the reasons that these initiatives failed, but the fact that most of us are not very good at pacing ourselves also contributed to the problems. We are not, on the whole, very good self-regulators and, in any group of learners, there are big differences in motivation, time management and goal setting. These differences are often amplified when self-paced self-study forms a significant part of the curriculum.

Managing a class of students who are all moving at different speeds can be hard work, and research into the benefits of self-pacing is inconclusive to say the least. Self-paced learning may work for some, but not for all.

Learning is also personalized through attempts to cater to learners' individual needs and interests. Specific learning needs, so long neglected, may be helped through new digital technologies. Text-to-speech and speech-to-text applications, for example, can make learning material accessible to many learners who would otherwise have difficulty. Fonts, spacing, colour, and page layout can all be designed for learners with dyslexia.

Motivation and engagement may also be enhanced when learning is designed to reflect learners' individual interests in the range and choice of topics, material and media. Teachers, if they have enough time, can be very good at this. Algorithms to generate automated personal recommendations are less effective, unless they have huge amounts of data, and even then, often fall very short. A growing number of language learning programs offer some choice in terms of content, but costs mean that the choice is usually fairly limited. Quality materials need to be written, curated, formatted, updated, checked, and so on, and all this takes money.

Takeaways

The hype of personalized learning of the digitalised variety has been fuelled by many hundreds of millions of dollars of investment from Big Tech and associated philanthropic foundations. The learning returns on that investment have been slim. One research report, commissioned by one of the largest funders of personalized learning, only managed to find 'suggestive evidence' that digitalised personalization 'may' be related to learning gains (Pane et al., 2017). As an endorsement, it's less than ringing.

The *idea* of personalized learning is seductive, so long as it remains a little vague. The more we zoom in on the details, however, the less convincing some of them seem. Self-pacing, individualised goal-setting and catering to learner preferences are all possibilities to be explored, but it's unlikely that satisfactory 'solutions' can be engineered with technology. The dream of personalized learning raises more questions than it answers, but they are still important and interesting questions.

How, for example, can we best find a balance between individual and group needs and interests? How can we help our learners to acquire the skills that are needed for autonomous learning? Can we offer choices in the kinds of homework that we ask learners to do? How can we encourage the use of learning tools like vocabulary flashcards and automated feedback (see 24)? How can we best develop an awareness of learning strategies and metacognitive skills (see 28)?

Disick, R. S. (1975). *Individualizing Language Instruction: Strategies and Methods.* New York: Harcourt Brace Jovanovich.

Griffiths, G. and Keohane, K. (2000). *Personalizing Language Learning.* Cambridge: Cambridge University Press.

Pane, J. F., Steiner, E. D., Baird, M. D., Hamilton, L. S. and Pane, J. D. (2017). *Informing Progress: Insights on Personalized Learning Implementation and Effects.* Seattle: Rand Corporation retrieved from: https://www.rand.org/pubs/research_reports/RR2042.html

Adaptive technologies are used to automate personalized learning routes for online learners. Their use in language learning is fairly restricted, but the same technology is now widely used in language testing.

What and why?

The function of adaptive learning technologies is to personalize (see **18**) aspects of the online learning experience in order to make it more motivating and more efficient. Since personalized learning means different things to different people, the precise function of adaptive learning (i.e. what exactly is personalized) also varies from context to context. Broadly speaking, however, it can be described in the following terms. When learners interact with online learning material, they generate data about how accurately they respond, when, how often and how fast they are working, the order in which they work through the material, how their interaction patterns differ from or are similar to their peers, and much more besides. All or just some of this data can then be used to generate recommendations for what the learner should (or must) do next. The whole process is automated, dynamic and interactive, and may be supervised by a teacher who can personally intervene when appropriate.

The more data that is available for analysis (see **22**), the more reliable the personalized recommendations for individual learners will be – at least in theory. This means that adaptive systems should work best at scale. If an individual learner's data can be aggregated with that of thousands of comparable learners, it becomes more valuable, as more can be learnt from it. The paradoxical promise of adaptive learning is that it offers personalized learning on an industrial scale.

Adaptive learning is most widely used in academic subjects, such as mathematics, where it is relatively easy to break the target learning down into small, 'granular' chunks, where one thing or skill (e.g. addition) is mastered by the learner and measured by the system before another (e.g. multiplication) is approached. Learning is seen to be linear and cumulative. Language learning, however, is mostly rather different, since language learners don't simply master one sound, one tense, or one communicative situation and then move on to the next. It is a recursive, cyclical and very idiosyncratic process, and researchers find it hard to agree on its precise nature.

English language learning programs which employ adaptive technologies typically focus on those aspects of language which most readily lend themselves to measurement: knowledge of vocabulary and knowledge of grammar rules, especially. This can be easily done by using scales such as the English Vocabulary and Grammar Profiles (see 21) which allow us to assign numerical values to particular lexical or grammatical items.

Language *skills* (speaking listening, etc.) are much harder to measure: they do not lend themselves easily to the 'mastery model' of learning that adaptive technologies support. Much language use is interactive and spontaneous, and it is very hard to separate it from its communicative contexts for purposes of quantification. The same holds true for plurilingual and intercultural competence, which may be one of the key objectives of English language teaching in some contexts. It is also unlikely that the development of critical or creative thinking will be much helped through adaptive programming.

In practice

One of the most common uses of adaptive technology in language learning is in vocabulary apps. For the most part, these are memory trainers which determine the order and the frequency with which lexical items are presented to a learner. They encourage spaced repetition of these items to optimise the learning possibilities and they use elements of gamification (see 23) to motivate the learner. The tasks include matching words to meanings, matching audio recordings to written forms, and dictation of words and phrases. The learner's performance on these tasks is measured and this information feeds back into the system to determine what happens next.

For these apps to be effective, they need to be loaded with appropriate content: target items that are important for specific learner needs. With some apps, teachers and learners can load their own sets of items, along with definitions or translations. It is then fairly easy to combine out-of-class use of the app with activities for the face-to-face classroom. Flashcard apps with some degree of adaptivity and high visual and game appeal are also popular with some younger learners. But, at a level of B2 and above, these apps have little value unless the target items have been chosen for a very good reason. Learners would be better advised to spend their time reading and listening to English.

The other common use of adaptive technology is in testing. Algorithms determine both the order and degree of difficulty of test items based on the learner's response to previous questions. Test questions can become progressively more or less challenging in a very fine-grained way. Such tests can be used for both placement and proficiency purposes. Besides allowing for a greater precision of scoring, adaptive tests can be shorter (and therefore cheaper) than tests in a traditional format.

Takeaways

Adaptive learning technologies have been widely rolled out in American secondary and post-secondary contexts. However, adaptive learning has not turned out to be the magic bullet that had been hoped for. Some research has found that it led to improvements in learning outcomes (see 20) in subjects like mathematics, but, on the whole, the large research studies have been less than enthusiastic.

The recent history of adaptive learning does serve as a useful cautionary tale. Hyped as an engineered, high-tech 'solution' to education, it has so far failed to find much employment in language learning. Like other educational technologies, it delivered less than it promised, but eventually settled down and found a much more restricted use (in, for example, memory apps and testing) than initially anticipated. It certainly reminds us to be sceptical of claims that any given technology will radically transform learning.

Kerr, P. (2016a). *Personalization of language learning through adaptive technology*: Part of the Cambridge Papers in ELT series. [pdf] Cambridge: Cambridge University Press.

Kerr, P. (2016b). Adaptive Learning. *ELT Journal* 70/1: 88–93.

Outcomes and frameworks

Few would disagree that learning outcomes need to be measured, but we also need to remember that measurement is likely to change the things that are taught and learnt.

What and why?

The recent story of outcomes and frameworks in language learning starts at the end of the last century when the wider world of education developed a perceived need for greater accountability, efficiency and cost-effectiveness. This entailed rigorous measurement of learning outcomes. PISA rankings, a growth in standardised tests, school and university league tables, all backed up by detailed frameworks, are reflections of the shift towards this more managerial approach to education.

Teachers in so many different contexts have already become so used to thinking in terms of learning outcomes (that can be measured) that it's hard to recall a time when things were any different. In order to measure these outcomes, we need frameworks to describe varying degrees of competence in a variety of skills. These skills could be language skills, learning skills, digital learning skills, or 21st century skills (see 7), and there are frameworks for all of them, regularly updated and expanded.

Frameworks to evaluate language proficiency have existed since the 1950s, but the publication of the Common European Framework of Reference for Languages (CEFR) in 2001, with its 'can-do' statements and its levels (A1, A2, etc.), has had the most lasting, global impact on language teaching and assessment. The CEFR describes varying degrees of communicative competence in receptive, productive and interactive skills. Here, for example, are abbreviated descriptors for spoken interaction, at two different levels:

I can interact in a simple way provided the other person is prepared to repeat or rephrase things. (A1)

I can express myself fluently and spontaneously without much obvious searching for expressions. (C1)

Although widely accepted, the CEFR is not without its critics, who have questioned its scientific grounding, its sometimes vague wording, and its reliability in evaluating performances.

Teaching and, therefore, the teacher also need to be evaluated. Many teacher/teaching frameworks exist, including some specifically for English language teachers. The Cambridge English Teaching Framework and the British Council's CPD Framework for Teachers of English are interesting examples (see below).

In practice

In the years following the appearance of the CEFR, references to the outcomes of individual lessons or activities within these lessons became increasingly common in coursebooks and other learning material. To draft these outcomes (e.g. 'I can talk about people I know and their families'), writers like myself copy from the CEFR, adding occasional details. It's not a job that most writers enjoy. The problem is that we know that these 'outcomes' are often more desired than realised. Even if, after a lesson, there are measurable gains in the ability to, say, talk about people you know and their families, there is no guarantee that the gains will remain visible in the days and weeks that follow. Many stated outcomes are necessarily vague, open to different interpretations of degree. Just *how well* do you need to talk about people you know?

High-stakes examinations and coursebooks are labelled with CEFR levels. Policy decisions are made with reference to them and our own language skills as teachers may be evaluated by them. People began to use the labels by adding slash marks and plus or minus signs (e.g. A2/B1 or B2++) in order to differentiate the levels of the framework more finely. Taking this further, some tools allow for an even more granular scale (see **21**) where the six levels of the framework are spread out linearly and each language skill can be measured with a score (from 10 to 90 on one scale).

The years since the appearance of the CEFR have also seen a huge growth in the teaching of English to younger learners. This has usually been accompanied by the development of frameworks to measure the extent to which national goals are being met, and the way that language is described inevitably affects the teaching approach. The prioritised outcomes might, for example, be speaking and listening skills. Alternatively, vocabulary growth might be seen as the main target.

Language-outcome frameworks inevitably influence what language teachers do in a classroom, but our teaching can also be influenced (at least some of the time) by teacher evaluation frameworks. Most usually, these are written by employers (often, the state) and do not always differentiate one kind of subject teacher from another.

For English language teachers, both the British Council CPD Framework and the Cambridge Framework were designed for *teachers* to understand and plan their own professional development. They were presented as tools to help teachers think about where they are professionally and where they want to go next. But frameworks can be used for purposes rather different from their designers' intentions. It is distinctly possible that frameworks such as these are more often used to evaluate teachers than for teachers to evaluate themselves.

Takeaways

The logical extension of a strong focus on outcomes, and measuring them, is the educational theory of *outcome-based education* (OBE). OBE, you will not be surprised to hear, means rather different things to different people, but the common thread is that every aspect of the curriculum is informed by consideration of the intended learning outcomes of the students. OBE grew in popularity in the 1990s, in the US and elsewhere, but problems with its implementation soon became apparent.

Selecting or writing meaningful, relevant outcomes is no easy matter, as we saw with the ability to talk about people you know and their families. If there is any vagueness in the descriptors, and there almost always is, the measurement of the outcomes becomes less reliable. In an English language class, there may also be positive learning experiences which cannot be easily predicted or measured: gains in autonomy and motivation, for example.

Even if not in the 'hard' form of OBE, educational outcomes and frameworks to measure them are not going to go away any time soon. The genie is out of the bottle. For teachers, the question is do they use us or do we use them? Can we use frameworks to guide the planning of lessons and curricula, and to guide our own professional development? Or are we constrained by the frameworks to teach in particular ways that are not always of our choosing?

Teachers do not have to limit themselves to trying to teach pre-determined outcomes. Instead, we can prioritise the processes (rather than the products) of learning, especially the management of classroom interaction, that create *opportunities* for learning – even if we cannot say, in advance, what kind of learning it will be. In practice, we may not have to choose between outcomes- and process-based approaches. Finding the right balance is at the heart of what language teachers do.

British Council. (2015). *Continuing Professional Development (CPD) Framework for teachers*. https://www.teachingenglish.org.uk/article/british-council-cpd-framework

Cambridge Assessment English (n.d.). *Cambridge English Teaching Framework*. https://www.cambridgeenglish.org/teaching-english/professional-development/cambridge-english-teaching-framework/

Council of Europe. (2018). *Common European Framework of Reference for Languages: Learning, Teaching, Assessment: Companion Volume with New Descriptors*. Strasbourg: Council of Europe. https://rm.coe.int/cefr-companion-volume-with-new-descriptors-2018/1680787989

Nikolov, M. and Timpe-Laughlin, V. (2021). Assessing young learners' foreign language abilities. *Language Teaching* 54 (1): 1–37.

21 Language scales

> Tagging individual language learning items (vocabulary and grammar) to framework levels may be helpful as a guide to what needs to be learnt, but language scales need to be treated with considerable caution.

What and why?

Frameworks (see 20) tend to be organised around language skills: they describe what a user can do with language (in relation to pre-determined levels). The descriptors in the frameworks are often and unavoidably imprecise. Phrases like 'good control' or 'occasional slips' will be interpreted differently in different contexts.

Language scales, on the other hand, although they are very closely tied to frameworks, are organised around knowledge, and claim to be more objective. They ascribe a level-value (A1, A2, etc.) to individual language items like a word, a word meaning or a verb pattern.

Attempts to establish which words it makes sense for a learner to learn at different language levels go back a long way. The development of enormous digital databases of language (corpora), in the second half of the last century, made it possible to analyse the frequency of individual language items (words, tenses, etc.). Knowing how frequently an item occurs gives us useful information in deciding how valuable it is to learn. Dictionaries, based on these databases, tell us which words – and meanings of words – are most common, and which patterns are most often associated with individual words.

It is only a relatively short step to mapping this kind of information on to skills frameworks like the CEFR. The development of digital databases of English, such as the Cambridge Learner Corpus (CLC), produced by *learners* whose level had already been established, made it possible to match individual language items to the levels at which learners typically started producing them – to varying degrees of accuracy or appropriacy.

English Profile, a Cambridge project supported by the Council of Europe, draws on the CLC to recommend particular items of grammar and vocabulary that are suitable for teaching and learning at each level. Pearson's Global Scale of English (GSE), in addition to a large number of can-do statements, offers something similar. It breaks the CEFR levels down into sub-levels (e.g. A2+, B2+), and assigns a number corresponding to these sub-levels for each vocabulary or grammatical item.

These two scales were developed using different data, so we should not be surprised to find differences in the level assigned to different items. For example, the word 'level' is described by English Profile as an 'A2' word, whereas the same meaning of 'level' is described by GSE as a 'B2' word. It must be said that closer correspondences between these two scales are much more common than large differences. The noun 'profile' is B2 on one scale, B2+ on the other.

The relevance of a word's score to your own learners depends on which database of language the scale uses. Was the language produced by adults or by children? Was it spoken or written? Was it in an academic or professional context? The answers to these questions will significantly affect the kind of language in the database, so a scale produced by analysing the language of high-school students in a formal exam will be of limited value to an adult learner of the same level who uses English in her job as a paramedic for an international aid agency. There are scales that have been developed for younger learners and for students of academic English, but these categories are still very broad – too broad for learners with very specific needs.

In practice

Language scales, in particular in the form of lists of vocabulary items, are now widely used in designing and writing tests. Most tests, but not all, evaluate learners' *knowledge* of English, and the scales provide a checklist of the vocabulary and grammar knowledge that can be tested. Where there's a test, there's a washback effect, as teachers and materials teach towards the test.

Both English Vocabulary Profile and the Teacher Toolkit that accompanies GSE allow users to select a CEFR level, a topic and a part of speech to generate lists of words. These are words 'to be learnt', so materials producers (writers, editors and publishers) usually now make frequent reference to the lists when doing their work. Coursebook writers like myself are familiar with being told by an editor that a particular word or grammatical structure is 'above level' and must be removed from an exercise. I have also worked on the development of flashcard vocabulary apps, and the items on these are also now selected with reference to language scales. Other popular, more general, language learning apps, like Duolingo and Rosetta Stone, also tend to structure their content in line with language scales.

Teachers can also refer to the scales themselves directly, in selecting or preparing appropriate learning materials. One useful tool, which is simply a kind of interface with the scales, is a 'text checker' or 'text inspector'. These tools, like English Profile Text Inspector, allow you to identify words of a particular level and give some indication of the readability of the text.

Takeaways

Languages scales are certainly useful in the design of teaching and testing materials. They appear to offer objective reasons for including particular items, but they need to be viewed with caution. Here's why.

The idea that learners of a certain level should be able to recognise or produce a certain number of words or structures – and the higher the level, the more they know – makes intuitive sense and has been confirmed by researchers. Researchers, however, are interested in *average* numbers. Whilst the average B2 learner may know 3,500 words, there is considerable variation between individual learners at that level, and the more the scale is subdivided into smaller levels (or numbers), the more variation we are likely to find. Part of this variation can be attributed to the learners' first and other languages, since it is much easier to produce or recognise English words if they are similar to their equivalents in these other languages. In theory, scales could reflect this: in practice, they don't.

Things become even more messy if we attempt to specify which particular items learners need to know at any given level. Vocabulary development does not proceed in a step-by-step, incremental manner. Our breadth of vocabulary knowledge (the number of words we know) improves at the same time as the depth of our knowledge of those words (how those words collocate with other words, for example). This simply cannot be reflected in language scales, and the danger is that such scales blind us to the real challenge of vocabulary acquisition. Handy as these scales might appear, the nature of language learning is not as straightforward as they might lead us to believe.

English Profile http://www.englishprofile.org/

English Profile Test Inspector http://www.englishprofile.org/wordlists/text-inspector

Global Scale of English https://www.pearson.com/english/about-us/global-scale-of-english.html

Milton, J. and Alexiou, T. (2009). Vocabulary size and the Common European Framework of Reference for Languages. In: Richards, B., Daller, M. H., Malvern, D. D., Meara, P., Milton, J. and Treffers-Daller, J. (Eds.) *Vocabulary Studies in First and Second Language Acquisition*. London: Palgrave Macmillan.

22

Learning analytics

We need information about our learners in order to be able to support them most effectively, and learning analytics provides huge amounts of data. But it is the quality, more than the quantity, of this information that will determine its usefulness.

What and why?

Educational institutions and teachers have always collected and collated data about their students and their learning. They keep records of demographic information, about attendance, punctuality, and disciplinary issues, about formal grades and more impressionistic evaluations, extra-curricular activities, and so on. They are, essentially, collecting evidence (see 30), and they do this for a number of reasons, ranging from legal requirements and course (or school) evaluation, to the use of this data to inform the formative assessment and support of the students.

Teachers in face-to-face classes know a lot about their students, but this is often less the case when study is online. We can't actually see what our students are doing and teacher-student ratios can make it difficult or impossible to keep track of individuals. However, online study can compensate to some extent for the lack of direct, personal knowledge about our learners because the amount of data about them that can be captured rises dramatically.

In addition to the kinds of data that is traditionally stored, learning analytics can draw on information about the ways in which learners interact with their online study program. How often, when and for how long do students log in to their program? Which components of the program do they use or not use, where on the platform do they spend most of their time, and how do they navigate around the various course components? On a much more granular level, what kinds of mistakes do they make, how often do they listen to a listening task, which words do they look up? In short, every click or keyboard stroke can be logged. Potentially, cameras can also capture eye movements as a way of assessing attention and engagement. When many thousands of students are using the same platform, this amounts to a huge amount of data.

Data storage in the cloud is clearly much easier than paper records, and new technologies of 'data mining' make the analysis of all this data – finding meaningful patterns – faster and cheaper. Findings from the analysis of the data can be visually presented to learners, teachers and institutions through the use of dashboards, which typically compare one learner's performance with others.

In practice

Learning analytics has only been part of the educational landscape since about 2011. There has been very little research into the use of analytics in language learning and teaching, and most published papers on the topic discuss its potential more than its actual applications. Nevertheless, some common uses are already well-established.

The number of learners who drop out of online courses is usually much higher than for students in traditional settings, and low retention rates are of particular concern in higher education where online study is most often found. There are many reasons for the high attrition rate, social, motivational and technological, and a combination of these. Learning analytics can do little to address the root causes, but it can identify patterns of online behaviour which correlate with those of students who have dropped out of previous courses. When at-risk learners have been identified in this way, support may be provided, either through personal interventions from faculty or through automated messages delivered on the platform.

Even when there is not thought to be any danger of drop-out, the behaviour of stronger and weaker learners can be compared, so that support can be provided for the latter. One large-scale study of language learners in Europe (Gelan et al., 2018) found that more successful students logged on to their course more often and more punctually, did more work while they were there and did it in the intended order, and referred more often to reference pages before moving on to practice tasks. The findings were not altogether surprising, but the early identification of less-than-ideal learning behaviour certainly makes remedial action more likely to be effective.

Analytics can also be used to feed back into course and task design. The order of learning tasks may be changed, individual tasks may be added or removed, or made more or less challenging. The study quoted above found that most learners went straight to assessed exercises, neglecting valuable learning activities, such as the use of voice recording, when these did not impact on their scores. Insights of this kind allow materials designers to modify courses so that students are nudged towards learning tasks that lead to greater learning gains or greater engagement. Course developers, including Rosetta Stone and Babbel, use learning analytics in these ways, but, sadly, details are not publicly available.

Takeaways

Learning analytics is already a multi-billion dollar global industry which affects the lives of millions of learners. It has also attracted considerable criticism. On the whole, research has suggested that learning outcomes may be improved for some learners through analytics, but there is still a lack of evidence from robust, large-scale studies. In this light, critics point to a number of dangers that come with the approach. The first of these concerns the security of the data about learners that is stored. It is simply not possible to ensure that data breaches are avoided, that privacy is maintained, or that the data is not used in unethical ways for which it was not intended.

It is also argued that the data collected in language learning contexts often leads to only limited insights. It can tell us about vocabulary scores and grammatical accuracy, but these are only rough guides to the more important outcomes of fluency and communicative competence. In addition, much that would impact on the process of learning a language is not usually captured. This includes any activity outside the platform, such as on social media. Data of this kind, if included, might well lead to more valuable insights, but the privacy issues become greater.

Despite the concerns, learning analytics is here to stay and its reach will continue to grow. This means that we must develop our (both teachers' and learners') ability to critically interpret the presentations of data in dashboards. The role of digital literacy (see **10**) will be increasingly important. In turn, this raises vital questions for all teachers. How much do we need to know about our students? What kind of information is most useful? And how will this information be obtained, stored and shared?

Gelan, A., Fastre, F., Verjans, M., Martin, N., Jansenswillen, G., Creemers, M., Lieben, J. and Thomas, M. (2018). Affordances and limitations of learning analytics for computer-assisted language learning: a case study of the VITAL project. *Computer Assisted Language Learning*. pp. 1–26.

Prinsloo, P., Slade, S. and Khalil, M. (2021). *Learning Analytics: A Primer*. Burnaby, Canada: Commonwealth of Learning.

Selwyn, N. (2019). What's the problem with learning analytics? *Journal of Learning Analytics*, 6(3): 11–19.

Yu, Q. and Zhao, Y. (2015). The Value and Practice of Learning Analytics in Computer Assisted Language Learning. *Studies in Literature and Language*, 10(2): 90–96.

23

Gamification

The most familiar aspects of gamification, like points, badges and leaderboards, may offer short-term benefits for some learners, but insights from the success of popular games suggest that social interaction has greater learning and motivational potential.

What and why?

Gamification, the incorporation of various elements from games into language learning activities, is often differentiated from game-based language learning, the use of games (either commercial games for entertainment or those designed specifically for language learners) as a medium for language learning. There can, however, be considerable overlap between the two. The most commonly used gamification elements are probably points and badges (numerical or visual representations of a learner's progress through the material), which can be shown as scores, levels that have been achieved, or 'lives lost'. These 'rewards' may be supplemented by others, such as the use of leaderboards, where a learner's performance is compared with others, credits which allow an avatar to be modified, or the unlocking of a game or video clip which the learner can play.

In many language learning apps, rewards are linked to personalized goals. Users are encouraged to set themselves targets in much the same way as fitness apps – typically, the amount of time each day that will be spent doing the work, or the number of consecutive days when work is done. When these targets are met, rewards are given.

The point of these rewards and personalized goals is to motivate the learner to engage with the material and to spend more time on-task. Many commentators have observed that these are the easiest aspects of a learning activity that can be gamified, but also only the most superficially motivating. Commercial game designers have learnt that greater engagement is more likely to come when there is interaction with other players, as opposed to simply playing against the machine. It is the social element of game play, whether in the form of collaboration or competition, or both, that has a more lasting impact on motivation and engagement.

If materials designers want to facilitate more meaningful social interaction, they will need to do more than modify the content of traditional learning activities by adding points, badges and leaderboards. A more radical rethink of the content will be required, making it much more like popular video games. These often involve some sort of narrative, where players have to work collaboratively to explore a topic or solve a puzzle. In the process, they must use a variety of critical and creative thinking skills as they communicate in English. Richer learning opportunities arise because a learning activity is more game-based, rather than because elements of gamification are present.

In practice

Language teachers have long used gamification in technology-free classrooms in attempts to motivate their learners. I have used points and rewards systems, for example, to encourage extensive reading or to discourage the use of L1 in speaking activities. However, the growing use of digital technologies for language learning, many of which include gamification elements, has changed the learning landscape and the use of gamification has become normalised. The need to motivate learners who were home-schooling during the Covid pandemic has contributed further to this process, and it is probably in the use of apps for self-study that gamification is most frequently used.

Globally, the most popular language learning app at the time of writing is Duolingo. Its content has often been criticised, but its use of gamification is widely admired. This includes manageable daily goals for users, visual representations of progress with 'experience points' and badges, leaderboards, rewards in the form of a non-monetary currency which can be used to unlock special features, encouragement to follow friends, and discussion forums to interact with other users. There can be few, if any, developers of language learning apps who do not assume that gamification will be an important part of their product, and most will study Duolingo's approach as part of their design process.

A similar range of gamification elements can be found in flashcard apps (memory trainers), like Quizlet and Memrise, that are also popular with many language learners and teachers to promote the memorisation of vocabulary and grammar. Many other self-study apps use gamification, especially with younger learners, to motivate students to improve their spelling, to promote regular extensive reading (of graded readers), or to practise exam skills. These are often supported (and paid for) by national governments or international bodies like the EU.

Game-based quizzes, like Kahoot! Socrative and Wordwall, which can be used in both face-to-face classrooms and platforms like Google Classroom, are becoming increasingly common. A more ambitious use of gamification is found in behaviour management systems, like ClassDojo, which attempt to influence the social-emotional aspects of learning (see **13, 14, 15**), typically of younger learners. In these, students are given instant feedback, through a points system, for good classroom behaviour (e.g. punctuality, participation in group work, or not using the L1).

Takeaways

All teachers (I hope!) know that motivation is the most important nut that we have to crack. The big question, then, is the extent to which gamification might help us with our students. We know that many learners are more motivated when learning is more game-like, and the enduring popularity of collections of language learning games reflects this. But there has been very little research into how gamification elements like points, badges and leaderboards lead to language-learning gains.

What we do know is that the use of superficial motivational tools can be effective for some learners, but not all – some will find that the most common forms of gamification are juvenile or that they induce anxiety. We also know that these rewards can have a negative impact on the long-term intrinsic motivation that comes from finding the *learning* interesting or enjoyable. They are, therefore, best used in small doses over a short period of time. There is also a danger that rewards may encourage learners to spend too much time on one particular activity type. There are better ways of studying than spending hours on a flashcard app every day in order to work your way up the leaderboard.

Gamification may offer a quick, but temporary, fix to motivational issues, but the real lesson to be learnt from all of this is that, as Paul Driver (2012) observes, language learning is better served by exploiting the more fundamental features of successful games, where playful freedom, intrinsically motivating tasks and social interaction are prioritised.

Dehghanzadeh, H., Fardanesh, H., Hatami, J., Talaee, E. and Noroozi, O. (2019). Using gamification to support learning English as a second language: a systematic review. *Computer Assisted Language Learning*, DOI: 10.1080/09588221.2019.1648298

Driver, P. (2012). The Irony of Gamification. *In English Digital Magazine 3*, British Council Portugal, pp. 21–24 http://digitaldebris.info/digital-debris/2011/12/31/the-irony-of-gamification-written-for-ied-magazine.html

Kapp, K. M. (2012). *The gamification of learning and instruction: Game-based methods and strategies for training and education*. San Francisco, CA: Pfeiffer.

Reinhardt, J. (2019). *Gameful Second and Foreign Language Teaching and Learning*. Cham, Switzerland: Palgrave Macmillan.

24

Automated feedback

Automated correction and scoring are now widely used in international English language exams. However, the automation of feedback for learning, as opposed to grading, has advantages and disadvantages.

What and why?

Giving learners feedback on their work is a key part of a teacher's job, and it can be a very time-consuming one. Attempts to automate this task, in order to free up teachers' time for other things, go back to at least the 1960s when 'teaching machines' were developed that could automatically mark a learner's production of language forms. There were both technological and theoretical challenges, and the machines never really caught on. However, with recent, huge advances in digital technology, hopes for a technological solution to the feedback problem have been reignited, even though the theoretical issues have not gone way.

The important role that feedback plays in learning is well-established. It is also generally accepted that feedback which encourages learners to modify their language output (formative feedback) is a more powerful driver of learning than feedback which simply evaluates language output with a score, often in a formal test (summative feedback). But there is less agreement on what kind of formative feedback is most conducive to learning. This question has been the focus of debate for hundreds of years, and of research for decades, without any firm conclusions being reached.

Should feedback concentrate on learners' errors (corrective feedback) or would it, as some have argued, be more beneficial to give feedback on what learners have done well? What kind of balance between corrective and non-corrective feedback is likely to be optimal? In the case of corrective feedback, will learners benefit more from information about grammatical and lexical errors, or (in the case of their writing) from feedback on the content and organisation of their work? If the former, does direct, explicit feedback (when learners are told what is wrong and what the correct form should be) lead to more learning gains than indirect, implicit feedback (when learners are given prompts and encouraged to self-correct)? And, again, what kind of balance between implicit and explicit corrective feedback makes most sense? Is it even possible to offer generalised advice, putting aside differences between individual learners, learning contexts and particular learning tasks?

Lacking clear answers to questions such as these, developers of digital language learning programs tend to ignore them altogether and allow themselves to be guided primarily by what the technology can do best.

In practice

It is a relatively straightforward matter for materials designers to automate learning tasks for which there is only one or a very small number of correct answers. Tasks such as gap-fills, multiple-choice and matching exercises, usually focussing on vocabulary or grammatical accuracy, lend themselves easily to automated correction. Unsurprisingly, this kind of work usually forms the backbone of language courses where learners work independently and where corrective feedback needs to be automated.

These tasks are basically tests of language knowledge. Whilst practice tests are known to help learners in memorising information, especially in the building of vocabulary, they are likely to be of more value when the feedback prompts them to self-correct, rather than simply providing right/wrong responses, along with the correct form when a mistake has been made. The most common and partial solution to this is for the program to generate dialogue boxes in response to errors, in which learners are encouraged to refer again to reference material. However, this is not always specific enough to be truly helpful, and it is not especially motivating either.

The practice of pre-determined items of vocabulary and grammar in pre-written sentences or short texts may be popular, but learners will benefit more from feedback on more extended language (writing and speaking) that they have produced more freely. The technological challenge here is much greater, but the last ten years have seen enormous progress in our ability to detect written errors in text (see, for example, *Write & Improve*). Spelling mistakes are probably the easiest to identify automatically, but certain kinds of grammatical error (including subject-verb agreement and part of speech) and problematic lexical collocations can also be highlighted with varying degrees of reliability. Depending on the kind of text, the reliability of error identification may be over 90 percent, but it now seems unlikely that software will ever, with 100 percent certainty, be able to determine whether a section of text contains errors or what kind of errors they are. It can, however, indicate probabilities.

Part of the problem is that reliable correction often depends on evaluating a writer's intentions. Teachers can often guess what kind of meaning a writer wanted to express, but automated feedback operates mostly by analysing sequences of words. It does not actually 'understand' anything. For this reason, it can say very little about the content and organisation of a piece of writing.

With spoken language, the challenges are even greater, since the system first uses speech-to-text software to convert the speech into written form, and, as anyone who has used a voice assistant on their phone knows, the results can sometimes be some way off the mark. With both written and spoken texts, the program compares the language that a learner has produced with a database of 'acceptable' language. It is therefore inevitable that such programs struggle with certain varieties of English, which may be perfectly appropriate in some contexts. Consequently, it is hard to see how automated feedback could ever be used, for example, with plurilingual practices (see **1**).

Takeaways

Gap-fill-style practice of grammar and vocabulary may have some value in preparing students for certain kinds of test, but whether it can lead to the development of fluency is questionable. Having said that, if learners are to follow a substantial diet of such work, most teachers will welcome the automation of feedback/correction as it saves them from the endless and dispiriting task of correcting reams of printed exercises.

Automated feedback on more extended written work offers, in my view, much greater potential. The focus on accuracy means that there is a risk of neglecting what is arguably of greater importance – content and organisation – but in approaches to the teaching of writing where students work collaboratively through a series of drafts, automated feedback may be effectively combined with other kinds of feedback. In early drafts, learners concentrate first on content and organisation, and receive feedback from the teacher or their peers. In later drafts, automated feedback on accuracy can be deployed. The technology can, therefore, complement the teacher's work, but it cannot replace it.

Cambridge English *Write & Improve*. https://writeandimprove.com/

Heift, T. and Schulze, M. (2007). *Errors and Intelligence in Computer-Assisted Language Learning*. New York: Routledge.

Kerr, P. (2020). *Giving feedback to language learners. Part of the Cambridge papers in ELT series*. [pdf] Cambridge: Cambridge University Press. Available at: https://www.cambridge.org/gb/files/4415/8594/0876/Giving_Feedback_minipaper_ONLINE.pdf

The potential of chatbots in education is often hyped, but useful applications of the technology remain limited. It seems unlikely that they could ever replace human conversation as a driver of language acquisition.

What and why?

There is little doubt that extensive opportunities for meaningful, communicative interaction play a vital role in the development of a learner's language skills. This interaction can be with a teacher, other learners in pair and group work, or, more informally, in conversation with any speaker of English. Conversational interaction allows for intensive spoken language practice, as well as exposure to the language produced by the interlocutor. For a variety of reasons, however, language classrooms may not always offer many conversational opportunities, and, even if they do, some learners may be reluctant to make the most of them. What's more, all learners could benefit from more frequent opportunities for conversation outside the classroom.

One way of meeting this need, it has been suggested, is for learners to interact with chatbots – sophisticated computer programs that can simulate, to a greater or lesser extent, a conversational partner. Similar to virtual assistants like Amazon Alexa, most chatbots can decode spoken words and respond with human-sounding voices. The obvious advantage for language learners is that they can be used any time, anywhere, if you have a reasonably up-to-date phone and a good connection.

Enthusiasts also point to other advantages of chatbots. Unlike humans (teachers, fellow students), they are non-judgemental, and this may help the motivation of shyer learners, some of whom may prefer to practise spoken language independently before trying things out with a live interlocutor. They may also appeal to those lacking in confidence, who are negatively affected by the fear of making language errors. Besides the absence of social pressure, there is no time pressure, either. Learners can take as long as they like for each conversational turn, allowing them to prepare or rehearse what they want to say. Chatbots do not get bored or lose patience. Many of them can interact with both text and speech, and allowing learners to choose the channel of communication (or to opt for both spoken and written at the same time) offers further potential advantages.

Virtual assistants are now so widely used in daily life that interaction with a chatbot does not seem strange or alienating to many learners. Research in educational settings (Fryer et al., 2020) suggests that many learners are not only ready to use and trust chatbots, but that some prefer them to a human partner. Although the novelty effect inevitably wears off, chatbot developers claim that the artificial intelligence engines inside the program can learn from previous interactions, and, as a result, interactions become more interesting and more engaging the more that the app is used. Combining chatbot technology with virtual reality (see 26) or elements of gamification (see 23) may also lead to enhanced engagement.

In practice

Recent years have seen enormous advances in Artificial Intelligence (AI) and Natural Language Processing (NLP), the two technologies behind chatbots. However, we are still some way off from having a machine that can truly understand human language, and this means that chatbots cannot really simulate a human conversation partner. Brief exchanges are usually unproblematic. The chatbot basically responds to lexical items and grammatical patterns, but it struggles to take account of the broader discoursal context, and, as a result, fails to respond in an appropriately empathetic way. This soon leads to breakdowns, as in the example below of a conversation with a chatbot that I had, where the illusion of communication and the interest of the user are both lost.

Me: Guess what happened to me on the way to work this morning.

Chatbot: What happened?

Me: I got knocked off my bike.

Chatbot: By who?

Me: It was a bus.

Chatbot: What did he do to her?

Chatbots are much more effective and convincing, in both the real world and in educational settings, when they are used in relatively brief exchanges of a transactional nature, where the content and the conversational turns are reasonably predictable. In the real world, these exchanges often involve some kind of marketing or customer support, such as following or preceding a purchase or a booking. Examples include those developed by food stores to help people find a recipe, by health authorities to give information about vaccinations and medical tests, or by educational institutions to provide answers to administrative enquiries.

These bots can provide useful authentic practice for language learners of the kind of language that features in the 'functional language' or 'everyday English' strands of most coursebooks. The practice is mostly limited to listening or reading, but feedback on the learner's language production is only indirect and only if the chatbot fails to understand what has been said or written.

There have been attempts to develop chatbots specifically for language learning that can provide feedback on the accuracy or lexical variety of the users' language. However, these are more like interactive tutorials than meaningful conversations, and attempts to provide reliable, automated feedback are fraught with challenges (see **24**).

Takeaways

Practice of structured, situational dialogues has been a feature of language learning and teaching for centuries and remains so today. When I began teaching, this kind of work was carried out in the language laboratory or with cassettes for home study. Chatbots that facilitate this practice are more user-friendly in that they can be easily incorporated into existing, familiar technology (e.g. social media). They are also more flexible, allowing for more than one possible response, and they may provide some useful feedback. Their value is, however, mostly restricted to lower level learners.

The use of this technology to practise limited conversational routines is a far cry from the claims of some that chatbots driven by AI will radically transform language learning by offering opportunities for communicative interaction that is indistinguishable from human conversation. Most researchers agree that if such technology ever arrives, it is still decades away.

Dokukina, I. and Gumanova, J. (2020). The rise of chatbots – new personal assistants in foreign language learning. *Procedia Computer Science* 169: pp. 542–546.

Fryer, L. K., Coniam, D., Carpenter, R. and Lapusneanu, D. (2020). Bots for Language Learning Now: Current and Future Directions. *Language, Learning and Technology* 24(2): pp. 8–22.

Lee, J.-H., Yang, H., Shin, D. and Kim, H. 2020. Chatbots. *ELT Journal*, 74 (3): pp. 338–344.

26

Virtual reality (VR)

> For many years, enthusiasts have been talking up the
> potential of VR for language learning. But even with more
> sophisticated and cheaper technology, language learning
> gains remain elusive.

What and why?

The term *virtual reality* (VR) is often used very loosely, and what
is described as VR comes in many shapes and sizes. A common
categorisation breaks it down into two main types: non-immersive and
immersive (Lan, 2020).

The former involves a simulation of physical space, shown on an
ordinary screen, which the participants can navigate, usually in the form
of an avatar. The immersive variety requires a head-mounted display
(HMD), headphones and (often) body sensors, and allows participants
to feel much more part of the virtual world they are exploring.

An example of a non-immersive virtual world is *Second Life*, launched
in 2003, which allows people to wander around a simulated world,
meeting others as they go. It soon found enthusiasts among language
educators, because of the (at least initial) immersive nature of the
experience and because of the opportunities it offered for interactive
communication. A number of virtual schools were set up in *Second Life*,
where lessons could be offered much as in the non-virtual world, but it
was also possible to chat with others more informally while exploring
the virtual world. More fully immersive virtual worlds, dedicated
to language learning, now exist. Making use of other technological
developments, participants can now interact not only with other people,
in the form of avatars, but also, by using natural language processing
tools (such as speech recognition), with automated bots (software which
simulates a conversation partner).

In addition to the above, VR is also sometimes used to describe the
experience of using simple and relatively cheap headsets, like a simple

3D viewer, combined with headphones, to explore both real and simulated worlds captured with 360° photography.

Early investment in VR led to the development of products for aviation, medical and military training, where the virtual world offered obvious advantages of physical safety. Entertainment applications soon followed, and it was this that probably most inspired language educators to look for ways of using VR. It was hoped that language learners, if fully absorbed in a virtual world, would be more closely engaged with the learning material. If using an HMD, learners would be effectively forced to engage with the material, since their gaze could not wander elsewhere (Bonner and Reinders, 2018)!

Motivation, then, is the key factor behind calls for wider use of VR in language learning. True, learners can interact and collaborate communicatively, and authentic situations can be simulated, but these aims can be achieved without VR.

In practice

After an initial flurry of enthusiasm, interest in the use of virtual worlds like *Second Life* declined, both from ordinary non-educational users and from educators. It needed powerful hardware and was not easy to use. Attention shifted towards the creation of virtual worlds specifically designed for language learning, and a growing number of products are available. In these, learners typically practise functional language in everyday situations, either by interacting with a chatbot or a filmed actor.

The potential of digital games for informal language learning has long been recognised. The range of VR games available is growing fast, as is the number of gamers using VR headsets. When these are multi-player games, users may socialise, negotiate and collaborate as they complete tasks in their quests. Some teachers have successfully incorporated such games into their classroom practice, adopting a task-based approach.

There are ongoing projects to develop similar VR games specifically for language learners, where the language demands of the tasks may be better calibrated. However, development costs are high, making it extremely difficult to match either the immersive or the gaming experience of products with investments of hundreds of millions of dollars.

Since the more immersive forms of VR require learners to wear HMDs, effectively isolating them from the rest of the world, they do not obviously lend themselves to classroom use. However, when only a limited number of headsets are available, information gap activities can be set up. The learner who is interacting with the virtual world communicates what they are experiencing with partners. This is possible with cheap equipment like a phone and a 3D viewer to view 360° photography, where learners can explore anything from a museum or a Disney castle to a coral reef or outer space.

Takeaways

Despite their learning potential, for reasons of preference or cost, video games are not for everyone. As the novelty effect wears off, the motivational pull declines, since the immersive potential of VR is as much (if not more) a feature of the intrinsic interest of the simulated world as it is of the technology that is used for presentation. The incorporation of VR in language learning materials does not diminish the central importance of providing interesting content. When you strip away the VR from the commercially produced language-learning packages, they often stand up poorly in comparison to comparable printed books and videos, which can be updated much faster and more cheaply.

An often-overlooked aspect of the appeal of VR in entertainment is that users have chosen voluntarily to take part. In educational settings, this exercise of free choice is less likely to be the case. In entertainment, too, continued engagement within the game is often the result of features of game design that allow for autonomy within the game: flexibility in the choice of goals and the strategies that can be deployed in achieving them (Ryan et al., 2006). Again, this is largely absent from the commercially-produced packages that are currently available.

In addition, the range of learning materials available is relatively limited, mostly appropriate for levels A1 to B1, and for reasons both commercial and technological, higher levels are likely to remain relatively uncatered for. At higher levels, too, VR packages that rely on bot technology will allow for only limited meaningful interaction (see 25). Still, for self-study, and for those who do not find HMDs uncomfortable or disorienting, there will be learners, especially at lower levels, who will be attracted to a VR approach.

Perhaps, the most useful lesson to be learnt from attempts to use VR in language learning concerns the need to promote lasting engagement (see **13**) in the learning process. There are no easy, one-off solutions out there to this – one of the biggest educational challenges.

Bonner, E. and Reinders, H. (2018). Augmented and virtual reality in the language classroom: Practical ideas. *Teaching English with Technology*, 18(3): pp. 33–53.

Lan, Y. J. (2020). Immersion, interaction and experience-oriented learning: Bringing virtual reality into FL learning. *Language Learning & Technology*, 24(1): pp. 1–15.

Ryan, R. M., Rigby, C. S. and Przybylski, A. (2006). The Motivational Pull of Video Games: A Self-Determination Theory Approach. *Motivation and Emotion*, 30: 344–360.

27

Augmented reality (AR)

> With its immediate, but superficial, appeal, AR has been
> promoted as a tool to revolutionise language learning,
> but practical and pedagogical limitations mean that it is
> unlikely that it will be widely adopted.

What and why?

Augmented reality (AR) is an interactive technology which allows
additional information to be superimposed on the real world when
viewed through the camera of a mobile device. Among the most well-
known AR apps are *IKEA Place* and *Pokémon GO*. The former allows
users to place potential furniture purchases in the rooms of their own
homes, in order to help them make their purchasing decisions. The
software 'reads' the 3D shape of both the object and the room, allowing
them to be combined. The latter is a game, using GPS technology, in
which players roam around the real world, hunting for Pokémons (3D
cartoon creatures) which can only be seen on their screens. Both of
these have been used by language teachers. Think of prepositions of
place and furniture vocabulary for *IKEA Place*, and of the possibilities
for meaningful communication between co-players for *Pokémon GO*.

Of more widespread use for educational purposes is a simpler AR
technology, called 'marker-based AR'. This uses static images (often a
basic outline or a QR code) to trigger the generation of the additional
information, which can be in the form of a written text, an image, an
audio or video file, or an animation. These triggers can be printed off
and displayed around the classroom, or, as is increasingly common,
included in books and other educational material.

The main reason for using AR in language learning and teaching is
undoubtedly its potential to motivate and engage learners by offering
fun and enjoyment, at least until the novelty effect wears off. A
second important benefit, depending on the particular app that is
being used, is that collaboration and communication between learners

may be fostered while they are involved in engaging tasks. The third potential advantage is that AR may allow for more authentic and richer multimodal content than would otherwise be possible. This may be especially helpful in CLIL settings (see **4**) or in classes where the development of intercultural competence is an important aim.

In practice

Probably the easiest way to use AR is in the learning of vocabulary for younger learners and lower levels. Commercial packs containing images of target vocabulary can be bought, and when the camera points at the image, the app generates the written form of the word, an audio recording, or an animated 3D version of the image. In order to overcome the limitations of pre-determined lexical sets, which may not be appropriate for particular classes, it is possible for teachers to create their own, although the software may not be free and the process is inevitably time-consuming. Some learners will undoubtedly enjoy this kind of approach, but there is a danger that they will be distracted by the technology and learning gains will not compensate.

Partly as a way of offering more supplementary material on a page, some published materials are now incorporating AR triggers. The digital material that is generated from them can be additional worksheets or practice test items, answer sheets, or, as in the case of a recent writing project of mine, video recordings of students carrying out a speaking task that can be used as either preparation or follow-up for the students in the class performing the same task.

Using apps that allow for the creation of AR overlays, some teachers have used book covers (e.g. of graded readers) as triggers so that students can read reviews or find out additional information before making their reading selection. Taking this a step further, students may record or write their own reviews, which are then made available for others. The addition of supplementary content (written, audio or video) to image triggers can also be used to provide integrated skills practice. For example, images of geographical locations link to further media about them. This is then used to plan an itinerary of a virtual tour.

AR has also been used when learning is taken out of the classroom, using GPS rather than image triggers. Hockly (2019) reports a number of projects where students explore and learn about their university campuses, by pointing their phone cameras at specified locations and reading more about them.

Takeaways

It is often said that a clear idea of pedagogical purpose needs to come before a decision to use any technology in a learning activity. The most obvious reason to use AR in language learning is its possible motivational pull, but against this we need to consider just how strong that pull might be. At the same time, a number of other questions, common to most uses of educational technology, need to be raised:

- Is there any convincing research evidence (see **30**) that suggests that this technology will lead to learning gains?
- Do all learners have access to appropriate phones and are wifi connections adequate?
- Are there any privacy issues involved in the use of the technology?
- Given that mobile phones can lead to classroom management problems, is there a sufficiently strong reason for this use of them?
- Will the use of this technology meaningfully enhance the digital literacies of your learners (see **10**)?
- Is the time (and sometimes money) that is required to learn to use the technology effectively a good investment? (For AR, the free software recommended by both Hockly (2017) and Wilden (2017) is no longer available.)

Godwin-Jones, R. (2016). Augmented reality and language learning: From annotated vocabulary to place-based mobile games. *Language Learning & Technology*, 20(3): 9–19.

Hockly, N. (2017). *ETpedia Technology*. Hove, UK: Pavilion Publishing.

Hockly, N. (2019). Augmented reality. *ELT Journal* 73(3): 328–334.

Parmaxi, A. and Demetriou, A. A. (2020). Augmented reality in language learning: A state-of-the-art review of 2014–2019. *Journal of Computer Assisted Learning*, 36(6): 861–875.

Wilden, S. (2017). *Mobile Learning*. Oxford: Oxford University Press.

> *Metacognition,* an awareness of one's own thought
> processes in learning, correlates strongly with language
> learning success. Training learners in metacognitive
> skills is therefore often recommended as a high-impact
> intervention which costs very little.

What and why?

Language teachers have long been interested in understanding the
characteristics of successful learners. Such learners have a high degree of
autonomy: they know their strengths and weaknesses, they know what
they want to achieve, and they know how to go about learning it. They
are, in other words, self-regulated.

In order to be self-regulated, they need three interrelated things. First,
they need to have at their disposal a range of cognitive learning skills,
such as knowing how best to memorise vocabulary or plan a piece of
writing. Second, they need metacognitive skills – the ability to plan,
monitor and evaluate their learning. Precise definitions of metacognitive
skills vary to some degree between different writers and the difference
between these and cognitive skills is not always crystal-clear. The final
ingredient in the mix is motivation – the desire to apply their cognitive
and metacognitive skills (see **13** and **14**).

Interest in strategy training for language learners is not new, going back
to at least the 1980s. But its importance has increased in recent years
as discussions of 21st century skills (see **7**) and the need to prepare
learners for a life of learning have brought the importance of cognitive
and metacognitive skills into sharper focus. Many would argue that
the whole point of language teaching is really to develop students into
lifelong learners. Metacognitive skills can help learners along this path.

Self-regulation and metacognition are also of more importance
now than ever before with the increasing numbers of learners

studying online, whether fully or partially (see **11**). Without effective metacognitive skills, the chances of course completion, and success, are much diminished. There is, then, an urgency in ensuring that all learners are equipped with these pre-requisites of successful learning. Unsurprisingly, metacognitive skills are now investigated in the Programmes for International Student Assessment (PISA) carried out by the OECD and feature prominently in their latest educational blueprint, 'The Future of Education and Skills 2030'.

In practice

Classroom training in metacognitive skills is often combined with work on listening, speaking, reading or writing. In the context of listening, Christine Goh (2008) has suggested a series of activities to develop both cognitive and metacognitive knowledge and strategies which she divides into 'experiential listening tasks' and 'guided reflections'. The first group includes things like:

- guidance prompts for learners to help in preparing for a listening task and evaluating how well they carried it out
- learners working with 'buddies' to identify listening resources and to discuss strategies for approaching them
- learners work together to design listening tasks for other members of the class.

The reflective activities include:

- diaries in which learners reflect on specific listening experiences
- learners use charts to record their affective responses to particular tasks
- learners evaluate their performance by filling in checklists of the strategies they have made use of (e.g. setting goals, drawing on background knowledge, guessing the meaning of unknown items).

In the context of speaking, Goh and Burns (2012) recommend a cycle of activities in which (1) learners prepare for a speaking task, (2) carry out the task, (3) focus on both language and strategies which would help improve performance on the task, (4) repeat the task, and (5) reflect on their performance, individually or in groups. The metacognitive training here uses similar activities to those suggested for listening work.

Incorporating metacognitive work in lessons where learners use language in a communicative way is a relatively simple matter. Researchers agree that regular short spurts of metacognitive work of the kind described here are more effective than entire lessons devoted to metacognition.

Takeaways

Unfortunately, my own experiences with metacognitive training have not been an unmitigated success. On a number of occasions, students have participated only reluctantly in metacognitive tasks and said they would prefer to spend time learning language than learning how to learn. They may have a point. Research into the value of metacognitive strategy instruction is 'hardly conclusive' and it seems that training in cognitive strategies is much more effective than metacognitive training (Plonsky, 2011). In other words, it may be more useful to spend additional time on training students to plan a piece of writing than on asking them to reflect on their use of this strategy.

One possible explanation for the mixed results of metacognitive interventions is that the relationship between metacognition and learning success is correlational but not causal. That is to say, it is possible that higher-achieving learners have better metacognitive skills because they are higher achievers, rather than the other way round. It is also clear that the effectiveness of metacognitive strategy training is very context-dependent: age, proficiency, educational setting, and the specific nature of the training will all affect outcomes.

My students were young adults taking part in short (ten-week) intensive exam preparation courses and their priorities did not include the reflective work that I wanted to promote. Their negative reactions might also, of course, have been due to the way that I taught them. I can, perhaps, find some consolation in the fact that some research has found that metacognitive training is usually more effective when done by researchers than by regular teachers.

While metacognitive training ought to bring benefits to learners, it will not necessarily do so. When time is limited, it might be better spent doing something else, such as training in cognitive skills, or anything else which learners find more motivating. Despite my own experiences,

I remain convinced that metacognitive training is worth exploring with some students in some contexts. But it now seems to me improbable that a few sweeps of a metacognitive wand will magically transform students into successful, self-regulated learners.

Education Endowment Foundation (2018). *Metacognition and Self-Regulated Learning: Guidance report*. London: EEF https://educationendowmentfoundation.org.uk/tools/guidance-reports/metacognition-and-self-regulated-learning/

Goh, C. (2008). Metacognitive Instruction for Second Language Listening Development. *RELC Journal*, 39 (2): 188–213.

Goh, C. C. M. and Burns, A. (2012). *Teaching Speaking*. New York: Cambridge University Press.

Plonsky, L. (2011). The Effectiveness of Second Language Strategy Instruction: A Meta-analysis. *Language Learning*, 61 (4): 993–1038.

Coaching has appeared in language teaching via the business world and coaching approaches are increasingly common with professional adults in private sector schools. However, the principles behind language coaching may be relevant to all language teachers, even though some of the practical applications may not always be feasible.

What and why?

Coaching, in both educational and corporate contexts, is a form of question-driven conversation, intended to help a learner or client to realise their potential, and is concerned with the development of autonomy and self-regulation (see 28). Language coaching is the incorporation of principles and practices from coaching into language teaching.

Coaches often structure coaching conversations in a similar way. Initially, they may ask the coachee to articulate their goals, both shorter and longer term in specific ways, and to reflect on the personal importance of achieving these goals. Drawing on common management practice, coaches may point coachees towards the importance of having goals that are specific, measurable, achievable, relevant and have a time-frame. Goals may be revised over the course of a number of coaching sessions. The focus then shifts to the current situation: how close the coachee is to the goals, what they are currently doing to achieve them and what resources they have available. Next, possible options for moving closer towards the goals are explored, along with the coachee's feelings about the different possibilities. This leads to decisions, which may also be later revised, about paths to be taken by the coachee.

This conversational model, referred to by the acronym, GROW, derived from its stages (goals, reality, options, way forward) is probably the most widely used, but there are many variations on it. No single definition of coaching and no single qualification is accepted internationally: as an unregulated field, anyone who wants to may describe themselves as a coach. Even in the world of language teaching, there are a number of different coaching organisations and there are enormous differences between them.

In practice

In ELT settings, the most obvious application of coaching conversations is in the process of conducting needs analyses (initial or ongoing), especially in the private sector with adults learning English for professional purposes. Unsurprisingly, this is where language coaching approaches are most often found. However, the influence of coaching may be seen more broadly and is described as coaching-informed, 'teaching in a coaching style' or as a mindset.

Coaching-informed teaching is often seen in opposition to traditional teaching styles where the teacher is primarily a transmitter of knowledge. Instead, with language coaches, the teacher's role is mainly facilitative: it is to 'help people learn rather than to teach them' (Barber and Foord, 2014). The focus is more on the learner than the teacher, and language coaching may be seen as a continuation of humanistic approaches that date back many decades (see **18**). This style of teaching is likely to contain the following elements:

- a focus on goals that are negotiated jointly between the teacher and the learners
- an acceptance that the teacher should be less of an authority figure and that there should be a significant degree of equality between teachers and learners
- a trust in the learner's ability to make appropriate decisions about their learning
- an acknowledgement of the central importance of the teacher as a motivator, confidence-builder and supporter of the learner
- a recognition of the importance of the learner's feelings towards the learning process
- a recognition of the role of the teacher as a listener who is genuinely interested in their learners as individuals
- an understanding of the role that a teacher's open-ended questions will play in shaping the dynamic of the classroom and in helping learners to reflect on their learning.

These elements will be reflected in the choice and organisation of activities in the classroom. Time is regularly set aside, for example, for learners to:

- develop a more concrete vision of themselves as effective language users and learners (see Hadfield and Dörnyei, 2013, for an extensive selection of practical suggestions)
- articulate their goals for both the course and for individual lessons and to self-evaluate the extent to which these goal have been reached
- decide what kinds of learning activities they want to take part in (including the amount and kind of homework they will do)
- articulate their emotional responses to their learning experiences
- explore, experiment with and evaluate different learning strategies and resources
- discuss and evaluate out-of-class learning activities.

When activities such as these are included in lessons and when time needs to be made available for individual coaching tutorials, it is inevitable that there will be less time for more stereotypical language teaching in the form of grammar and vocabulary instruction.

Takeaways

I have met very few language teachers who would not nod in approval when reading most (if not all) of the elements of coaching-informed teaching in the section above. The importance of motivation and goal-setting, the monitoring of progress, and the treatment of learners as individuals are rarely matters of debate. Language coaching, nevertheless, seems to divide opinion and the reasons for this deserve consideration.

Some teachers, not without cause, are sceptical about the whole unregulated world of coaching where hourly fees are often much higher than those that, say, a 'normal' language teacher can earn. Self-described language coaches may market themselves through an association with executive coaches, but there is an important difference. Executive coaches do not necessarily need to have any expertise in executive business functions. Language coaches must surely be considered charlatans if they have little understanding of language acquisition. Sadly, there are plenty of these around.

A few bad apples do not spoil a barrel, but there are other reservations about language coaching that colleagues of mine in a private language school have expressed. Some feel uneasy about taking on what they see as a counselling role, especially with learners who are older than themselves. Others feel uncomfortable about adopting a coaching style which they feel is culturally inappropriate or even unwelcome in some of their classes. However, the strongest reservation I have heard concerns the practicability of a coaching approach. For example, in large classes (especially in compulsory education) working towards a high-stakes examination, how much autonomy, equality or trust can realistically be expected?

The big question, then, that coaching raises for teachers is how we should balance what we believe to be good teaching with the institutional constraints we all work under.

Barber, D. and Foord, D. (2014). *From English Teacher to Learner Coach.* www.the-round.com

Guccione, K. and Hutchinson, S. (2021). *Coaching and Mentoring for Academic Development.* Bingley: Emerald Publishing.

Hadfield, J. and Dörnyei, Z. (2013). *Motivating Learning.* Harlow, UK: Pearson Education.

Kovács, G. (2022). *A Comprehensive Language Coaching Handbook.* Shoreham-by-Sea, UK: Pavilion Publishing.

Wade, P., Hunter, M. and Morrain, R. (2015). *Coaching & mentoring activities for ELT.* Smashwords.

D: Rethinking evidence

I have argued in the previous chapters of this book that we need to be cautious about the latest trends in English language teaching and I have often referred to research evidence as a reason for this. Much educational research, however, concludes that 'more research is needed'. Very little is fixed in stone, and we may be wise to maintain a sceptical approach to 'evidence', too.

---

30 Evidence

> It is obviously important that we have evidence to support what we do in our classrooms, but interpreting research evidence is, unfortunately, rarely straightforward.

What and why?

You won't have failed to notice the frequent references to research throughout the pages of this book and you will have probably noticed, too, that the research evidence that I talk about rarely provides unequivocal support for the trends under discussion. We shouldn't find this surprising, since it is in the nature of educational research that it must be interpreted in some way. It is rare that research findings can be generalised to the multiplicity of different local contexts in which teachers work. Conclusions, at best, are typically that this or that trend might or might not be worth exploring further.

Still, it is hard to disagree with the idea that language teaching could be more effective if it were more informed by research evidence, in the same way that medicine has embraced an 'evidence-based' approach in recent decades. This common-sense perspective is reinforced by the growth of an increasingly managerialist approach to global education practices, which requires evidence to justify the investments and policy decisions that are made.

We can divide the kind of research evidence that may usefully inform English language teaching into two broad categories: research into the language itself (how English is actually used) and research into how it is best learnt and taught, where experimental data, data from real classrooms and data from learners' interactions with learning software (see **22**) may all play a role. Published research into areas related to language teaching has recently seen explosive growth and growing specialisation, with the number of relevant journals estimated to be over 1,000. Since nobody could keep track of all this, syntheses of this research, known as meta-analyses or systematic reviews, have become much more common. Meta-analyses that investigate classroom teaching practices are basically interested in finding out what 'works' and what 'doesn't work', and calculate what is known as an 'effect size', a number that indicates the correlation between a particular teaching behaviour and academic achievement. The work of John Hattie (2009) is probably the most well-known and widely-cited example of educational meta-analyses.

In practice

Empirical corpus-based evidence about how English is actually used in the real world is now often used to shape learning materials. This usually involves consideration of the frequency of particular features of language in different kinds of discourse – words and phrases, grammatical patterns and aspects of pronunciation (see 21). Arguably, however, it is not used often enough, with much material still relying on an uncritical replication of earlier approaches or the uninformed intuitions of materials writers. But applying this evidence to course design is not a straightforward matter, and cannot be done without exercising value judgements. The kind of corpus that is used determines the insights that it generates, with an ELF (see 2) corpus and a British or American native-speaker corpus producing very different results. Preferring the latter over the former, for example, is a reflection of a set of values which it would be appropriate to uncover if it is not already explicitly stated.

Educational research raises even more questions than language research. Unlike medicine, where randomised controlled trials are the gold standard in determining whether a treatment works, such an approach is often not possible in education, for both ethical and practical reasons. It is often hard, if not impossible, to control for all the variables in educational settings, and even more so when key terms have not been adequately defined (as is the case with most of the trends discussed in this book). The result is that many experimental findings in second language acquisition need to be or cannot be replicated. Meta-analyses are, therefore, much less reliable than they might at first appear.

This is not to say that research evidence is of no value at all. For example, we know enough now to say, with some confidence, that the use of the learners' first language may be a help rather than a hindrance in learning another. We know, too, that the best kind of language practice is meaningful and communicative, and that corrective feedback can be beneficial. Good reviews of available evidence and its practical implications can be found in Ellis and Shintani (2014) and Boers (2021), or in a more teacher-friendly form in Lethaby et al. (2021).

But these insights tend to remain at the level of generalities. Precisely how, when or how often we should encourage the use of L1, provide communicative practice, or give corrective feedback is outside the scope of empirical research. This is extremely unfortunate because it is the answers to specific questions of this kind that teachers and materials writers most urgently need. It is often noted that teachers rarely read educational research, but, even if they did, they would not find much in the way of reliable, explicit guidance about what to do in their classes tomorrow. Instead, they will find ideas which could shape their general educational approach, although, over the long term, this is perhaps of greater value.

Takeaways

Most trends in ELT are promoted, at least initially, by those with vested interests – ideological or commercial – in them. The search for evidence in support of them comes as an afterthought. To catch on as an idea, a trend needs to be broadly, rather than narrowly, defined, and this looseness of definition leads inevitably to problems in establishing whether it 'works'. It is for this reason that we would be wise to adopt a sceptical attitude when evaluating claims that any addition to the scope of language teaching or any technology will radically transform the field, or will be appropriate to the contexts in which we work.

A better question to ask is, perhaps, what new trends work *for*. Whose interests do they serve? What values do they embody? Do we, for example, share the common assumption that the primary purpose of English language learning is to prepare our students for the twenty-first century workplace and that this training should be measured in terms of efficiency and efficacy? Can language learning be engineered to be more efficient? Do we believe that technology is an indispensable part of this training? Is the point of social-emotional interventions in the classroom mainly to improve learning efficiency, or is it more a question of basic humanistic respect and inclusivity? Can it be both?

We can only evaluate, in any meaningful way, the insights from research evidence by trying things out in our own classrooms, and I hope that this little book will encourage you to do that. At the same time, I believe that it would help us to explore further the values systems that underlie the various claims on our time. Unfortunately, I have no evidence to back up this claim: it is purely a value statement of my own.

Boers, F. (2021). *Evaluating Second Language Vocabulary and Grammar Instruction*. New York: Routledge.

Ellis, R. and Shintani, N. (2014). *Exploring Language Pedagogy through Second Language Acquisition Research*. Abingdon, UK: Routledge.

Hattie, J. (2009). *Visible Learning*. Abingdon, UK: Routledge.

Lethaby, C., Mayne, R. and Harries, P. (2021). *An Introduction to Evidence-Based Teaching in the English Language Classroom*. Shoreham-by-Sea, UK: Pavilion Publishing.

Index